This book belongs to
GRANDVILLE ASSEMBLY OF GOD

Who is coming?

You might ask that question as you glance at the title of this book. Who is coming? The author is looking for the coming of Jesus Christ, and he carefully examines Bible prophecies and present trends and events to support his views.

An important book in the light of current events.

Richard E. Orchard

GOSPEL PUBLISHING HOUSE
SPRINGFIELD, MISSOURI
02-0541

LOOK WHO'S COMING

Gospel Publishing House
Springfield, Missouri 65802

Library of Congress Catalog Card Number: 74-33870.

Printed in the United States of America

ISBN 0-88243-541-8

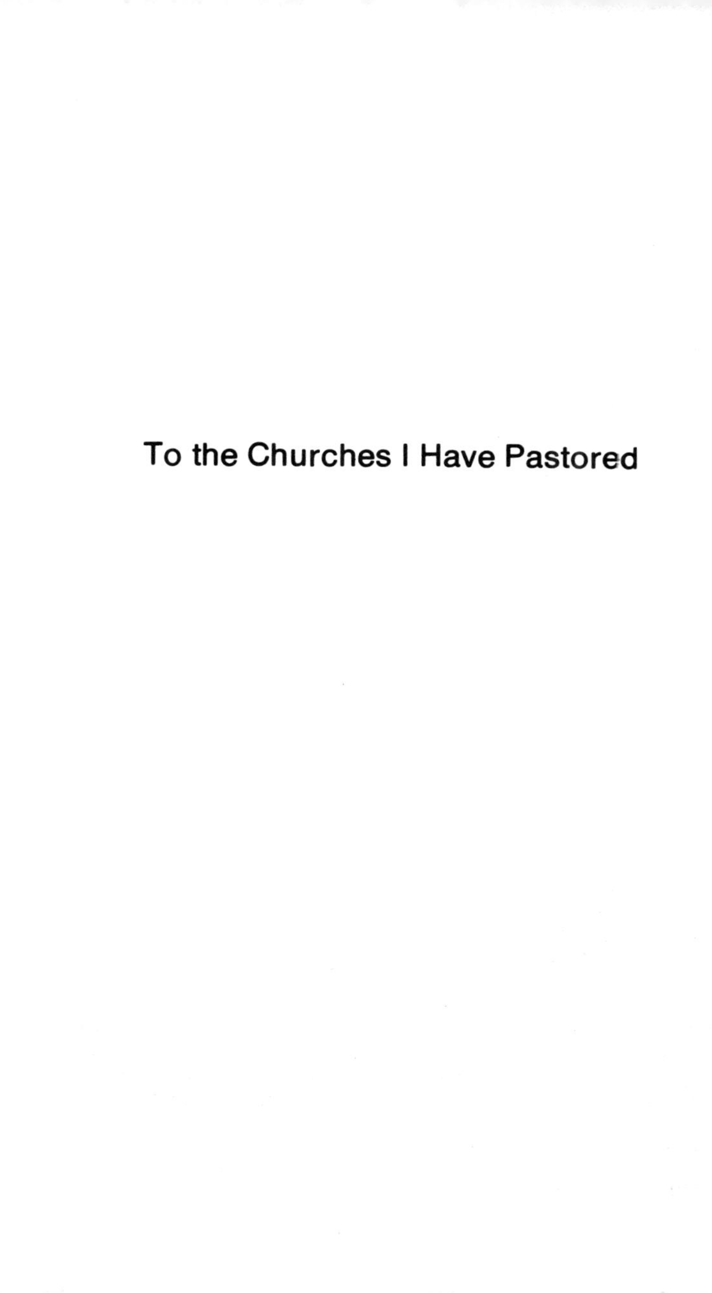

To the Churches I Have Pastored

Contents

Introduction

When Zacharias the priest received the communication from the angel that he and his wife Elizabeth would have a son, it was affirmed to him that this son would precede the coming of the Messiah.

> . . . many of the children of Israel shall he turn to the Lord their God. And he shall go before him in the spirit and power of Elias, to turn the hearts of the fathers to the children, and the disobedient to the wisdom of the just; to make ready a people prepared for the Lord (Luke 1:16, 17).

Such a communication was more than Zacharias could accept at the moment, and the angel said, "Behold, thou shalt be dumb, and not able to speak until the day that these things shall be performed, because thou believest not my words."

During the months spent waiting for their child to be born, the lowly priest pondered the angelic message, and no doubt searched the Scriptures concerning the amazing events about to take place. When his son was born he named him John, and, bubbling with inspiration, he declared,

> And you, my little son, shall be called the prophet of the glorious God, for you will prepare the way for the Messiah. You will tell his people how to find salvation through forgiveness of their sins. All this will be because the mercy of our God is very tender, and *heaven's dawn is about to break upon us,* to give light to those who sit in darkness and death's shadow, and to guide us to the path of peace (Luke 1:76-79, *Living Bible Paraphrased*).

Heaven's dawn is about to break upon us! The King James Version reads, "The dayspring from on high hath visited us," and the marginal rendering is, "The sunrising has come!"

Only a few months after the birth of John, another babe was brought to the temple for dedication, and an aging priest named Simeon, recognizing the Christ child by divine revelation, declared, "Lord, now I can die content! For I have seen him as you promised me I would. I have seen the Savior you have given to the world. He is the Light that will shine upon the nations, and he will be the glory of your people Israel!" (*Living Bible Paraphrased*).

By the tender mercies of God the dayspring has visited us from on high. The gospel light has taken us out of the darkness of pagan ignorance, and given us a meaning for the Old Testament types and figures. The truths about which we were utterly in the dark have been brought to light. Those who sat in the shadow of death like condemned prisoners have been brought a word of pardon. It is a light not only to our eyes, but to our feet also, guiding us into the way of making our peace with God.

One of the best attested facts of history is that God once visited this earth and walked upon it in the person of His Son. His coming was in the form of man, His demeanor that of a servant. People who knew Him marveled at His knowledge, and hung upon every word He spoke, for they agreed "never man spake like this man." His lineage and birth were documented in detail. After nearly 2,000 years the learned of this world are still endeavoring to plumb the depths of His teaching, and to fathom the mystery behind the amazing miracles He wrought.

He lived a most exemplary life for over 33 years, but His teachings and motives were misunderstood by envious and jealous princes of this world and He was brought to trial, a trial that will forever stand out as a judicial travesty. Though the trial judges found no fault in Him, He was sentenced to death by crucifixion, and died on a cross between two thieves. He was embalmed after the manner of the Jews, and laid in the tomb of a rich friend. On the third day He came out of that tomb, and for nearly six weeks appeared to many of His followers, encouraging and teaching them in view of their coming labors.

One day He was seen to quietly leave the earth and ascend into the heavens, and a cloud received Him out of their sight; and angelic messengers spoke to the crowd,

> Ye men of Galilee, why stand ye gazing up into heaven? this same Jesus, which is taken up from you into heaven, shall so come in like manner as ye have seen him go into heaven (Acts 1:11).

With the first coming of Christ into this world came the unfolding of the redemptive plan of God that was foretold and typified in the Old Testament. The first rays of heaven's dawn broke over a dark world as our Lord began to take out from among the nations a people for His name. The full blaze of God's glory upon the earth awaits the return of Jesus Christ from heaven to bring a final end to sin, to bring in everlasting righteousness, and to bring about the full culmination of those prophecies concerning the future glory of Israel, the divine rulership of the earth, and the eternal inheritance of the saints.

This book concerns that second coming of Jesus Christ to this earth.

1 The Coming of the Lord

A group of us were standing in front of one of Israel's war memorials located between the Hotel Intercontinental and the valley of the Kidron. Before us was the ancient wall of Jerusalem beyond which the Dome of the Rock stood shining in the sun. Down in the valley to our left was the Tomb of Absalom, and off to our right was the Garden of Gethsemane.

We were looking at a mixture of the very old and the very new, and a mixture of that which was authentic and that which was simply traditional. I knew that those walls had been rebuilt in the 16th century, and the ancient wall of Jerusalem beyond which the Dome sealed and was now guarded by an Arab cemetery. There was the corner of the wall known as "The Pinnacle of the Temple," which gets its height from the way the ground below falls away outside the Old City, but the temple itself had not existed since A.D. 70. Nearby was a grazing burro, and on the road behind us was a camel with its owner, a man who reminded us of an ancient patriarch. The entire scene was made noisy with the sound of 20th-century automobiles and buses, and I was aware of the fact that this city, above all others on the earth, had sacred places claimed by Protestants, Catholics, Orthodox, Muslim, and Jews.

It was while looking at this very historic city that one of the men nearby said, "Gentlemen, you are looking at the piece of real estate that is the cause of the energy crisis, and the cause of the distress among nations and international turmoil."

My mind went to the passage in Zechariah 12:2, 3, and the words of that ancient prophet suddenly came alive to my heart:

> Behold, I will make Jerusalem a cup of trembling unto all the people round about, when they shall be in the siege both against Judah and against Jerusalem. And in that day will I make Jerusalem a burdensome stone for all people: all that burden themselves with it shall be cut in pieces, though all the people of the earth be gathered together against it.

From the war memorial we took the path that led toward Gethsemane. The gate of an enclosure was open, and a friendly Franciscan priest met us and graciously offered to show us his garden and chapel. In obedience to his superiors, he lived there alone, guarding the grottos that had been excavated where the bones of early Christians had been found. He stated that we were standing on the traditional site where Jesus wept over Jerusalem.

I turned to face the city, and it seemed as though the Master was standing there once again, the tears upon His face, and I could hear Him say:

> O Jerusalem, Jerusalem, the city that kills the prophets, and stones all those God sends to her! How often I have wanted to gather your children together as a hen gathers her chicks beneath her wings, but you wouldn't let me. And now your house is left to you, desolate. For I tell you this, you will never see me again until you are ready to welcome the one

sent to you from God (Matthew 23:37-39, *Living Bible Paraphrased*).

Never again until . . . *until*—that was the word that seemed important to me at the moment. It was an implied promise to return to the city again, but not *until* great changes took place, especially in the attitude of the nation to whom He had once ministered. His ministry, when presented to this city and nation, had been rejected by all but a few loyal followers. The generation that followed Him saw slaughter and destruction such as no other generation had seen. In the siege of the city under the Roman Titus the holy temple was burned, flames licking the cedar work overlaid with gold—priests fell stricken with darts beside their own sacrifices—corpses lay in piles on the altar slopes and blood stood in lakes in the holy courts —gleaming mosaics were trampled—and crucifixions took place till there was room for no more crosses, and no more crosses for victims. Friends fought one another for grass or nettles to eat—miserable mothers, in the pangs of famine, devoured their children—1,100,000 men perished, and 97,000 were carried away captive, most of whom perished in entertainment arenas before wild beasts or at the hands of gladiators. Josephus, the historian, said: "Neither did any other city ever suffer such miseries, nor did any age ever breed a generation more fruitful in wickedness than this was, since the beginning of the world."

No wonder, then, that Jesus, foreseeing the coming horror, had wept and sorrowed as He thought how many times He would have sheltered them, and gathered them in love as a hen gathers her chicks, "but you wouldn't let me." Their house became a desolation, and He affirmed that they would see Him no more *"until you are ready to welcome the One sent to you from God."*

Nearly 20 centuries have gone by. Israel, in response to the call of the Spirit, has been responding from the ends of the earth to a restoration of their nation. Though they are regathered still in unbelief, yet Christian influences are being felt, and the prophetic Scriptures indicate their ultimate spiritual rebirth to an acceptance of their Messiah they once rejected.

Jesus is coming to earth again, and His feet shall once again tread the streets of Jerusalem, but His next appearance will not be amidst a rabble crowd of self-righteous who will shout "Away with Him, crucify Him," but rather the people of Israel will cry out, "Blessed is He that cometh in the name of the Lord."

2 The Promise of His Coming

The writers of the New Testament epistles were careful to devote a portion of their writings to answering the scoffers who doubt the integrity of God's Word and mock the doctrine of the second coming of Christ. Jude had planned to write about the salvation of God, and then changed his plans in order to put the saints on guard against godless teachers; and Peter had his eye on present conditions when he wrote,

> . . . in the last days there will come scoffers who will do every wrong they can think of, and laugh at the truth. This will be their line of argument: "So Jesus promised to come back, did he? Then where is he? He'll never come! Why, as far back as anyone can remember everything has remained exactly as it was since the first day of creation" (2 Peter 3:3, 4, *Living Bible Paraphrased).*

Peter was certain that the scoffers were "walking after their own lusts" and were afraid to face up to the fact they were headed for judgment. Their ignorance of God's truth was a willful thing, for a sufficient amount of evidence was available if they really wanted to know the truth.

An incident in the life of Dr. Samuel Johnson may serve to illustrate this truth. Being interested in writing and the literary arts he thought to join a society in Paris where writers presented their latest script before the club. Johnson learned that the members of this society were violently opposed to anything spiritual, and took every opportunity to speak against the Scriptures. So he laboriously copied the Book of Ruth from the Old Testament, making only a few deletions, and at the proper time read his manuscript before the members of the society. When he finished, the members were loud in their praise of such a beautiful piece of writing. "Where did you find such a beautiful theme?" they asked. "Where did you find such lovely names as Mahlon, Chilion, Naomi, Elimelech, and Boaz?" After listening to their comments and praises, Johnson said, "Men, you have been free through the years to criticize the Holy Scriptures and to belittle those who aspired to things spiritual; and it is indeed interesting to hear you praise my manuscript which came word for word out of the very Book you have hated but know so little about."

With that he laid his manuscript on the table and walked out, never to return. So it has been with the scoffers of all generations. A willful blindness has seized them. They speak against everything they do not understand, and are not interested in looking for any positive evidence that may change their minds.

The evidence for the second coming of Christ to this earth is overwhelming. It may be said that one of the major proofs of His second coming is the fact that He came the first time. The Holy Spirit inspired the writers of the Old Testament to set down over 300 promises relating to the birth of Christ, His life, ministry, trial, death, burial, and resurrection. All of those promises were fulfilled to the very letter, and the evidence of it is recorded in the four Gospels and in the writings of the Jewish historians. But the amazing fact is that more is said about the second coming of Christ in the Old Testament than about His first coming. This second group of predictions includes His appearing, His rulership over Israel, His judgment upon the nations, and many details concerning the coming conditions of earth under His leadership.

Add to the writings of the prophets the teachings of Christ himself, and the vast storehouse of material found in the New Testament epistles and in the Revelation, and one cannot help seeing that God's Son is due to return to this earth.

The first preacher in the Bible, Enoch, had a revelation of the Lord's second coming to earth:

> See, the Lord is coming with millions of his holy ones. He will bring the people of the world before him in judgment, to receive just punishment, and to prove the terrible things they have done in rebellion against God, revealing all they have said against him (Jude 14, 15, *Living Bible Paraphrased*).

Our Lord himself predicted His return a number of times in His teachings, and 1,900 years have gone by without its taking place. Many of us have been prone to ask, "Where is the promise of His coming?"

I was just a lad sitting under the ministries of Torrey Johnson, Old Brother Neve, and others when the message first came to my heart that Jesus was coming again. It was the late 1920's. America was heading into a disastrous depression, and the nations of Europe were still very much unsettled as a result of World War I. We were told to look for the Lord any day, any hour.

The decade of the thirties saw the rise of Mussolini and Hitler, and by 1939 Europe was plunged into another bloodbath which continued until 1945. We thought surely the Lord was at hand and expected

Him before the forties ended. But many more years have come and gone without His appearing.

Were we wrong to expect Him? Were we deceived into looking for something that was not to happen? No, we were not deceived. In our zeal and expectation we had perhaps forgotten that a day with the Lord is as 1,000 years and 1,000 years as one day, and what seemed long to us, in looking back over nearly 2,000 years of church history, was only a couple of days to our Lord. And James encourages us in our waiting for the Lord's return, when he said,

> Now as for you, dear brothers who are waiting for the Lord's return, be patient, like a farmer who waits until the autumn for his precious harvest to ripen. Yes, be patient. And take courage, for the coming of the Lord is near (James 5:7, 8, *Living Bible Paraphrased*).

Peter also reminds us:

> The Lord is not slack concerning his promise, as some men count slackness; but is long-suffering to us-ward, not willing that any should perish, but that all should come to repentance (2 Peter 3:9).

The promise of His coming is written in the hearts of those who have been truly converted to Christ. Such people have an inward expectation of Christ's return, a relationship to the Lord and to fellow Christians that has a sanctifying effect on their daily walk. After speaking about the coming of the Lord, Peter admonished all Christians to "be diligent that ye may be found of him in peace, without spot, and blameless." And when Paul spoke about the translation of the Church in 1 Thessalonians 4, he urged that we "comfort one another with these words."

The promise of His coming is written into the very theme of redemption, for the purpose of Christ's coming was to destroy the works of the devil, and the outcome of all prophetic utterance is that He must reign until all enemies are put under His feet and all traces of rebellion in God's universe are brought to a final end. It was an act of God's infinite love that He sent His Son into the world the first time to be the sacrifice for our sins and for the sins of the whole world. It will be an act of God's infinite mercy to have Christ come back to this world to usher in everlasting righteousness.

This was set forth so beautifully by the Psalmist in his second psalm when he portrayed the kings and nations of the world raging against the Lord and taking counsel against His program. He shows how the Lord laughs at the puny efforts of men to hinder His plan, and reaffirms the fact that the Son of God will ultimately sit upon the holy hill of Zion and the heathen shall be His inheritance, and the uttermost parts of the earth shall be His possession.

The promise of His coming was given by our Lord in many of His teachings. Upon that memorable occasion when He came to Jerusalem and wept over the city, He stated,

> Ye shall not see me henceforth, till ye shall say, Blessed is he that cometh in the name of the Lord (Matthew 23:39).

In His Olivet discourse the Lord portrayed the troubled times at the end of the Church Age—wars, rumors of wars, nation against nation, kingdom against kingdom, famines, pestilences, earthquakes, betrayal of one another, false christs and false prophets. He considered those days to be so terrible that if they were not shortened no flesh would be saved. Then after reciting the list of horrors about to fall on the world, He emphasized His return to the earth:

> For as the lightning cometh out of the east, and shineth even unto the west, so shall also the coming of the Son of man be. . . .
>
> And then shall appear the sign of the Son of man in heaven: and then shall all the tribes of the earth mourn, and they shall

see the Son of man coming in the clouds of heaven with power and great glory (Matthew 24:27, 30).

He declared that the day and hour of His coming was determined by the Heavenly Father. He was so anxious to get this truth into the hearts of His listeners that He repeated it again and again throughout the teaching of that day:

> But as the days of Noah were, so shall also the coming of the Son of man be (v. 37).
>
> Watch therefore; for ye know not what hour your Lord doth come (v. 42).
>
> Therefore be ye also ready: for in such an hour as ye think not the Son of man cometh (v. 44).
>
> Watch therefore, for ye know neither the day nor the hour wherein the Son of man cometh (25:13).
>
> When the Son of man shall come in his glory, and all the holy angels with him, then shall he sit upon the throne of his glory (25:31).

The promise of His coming was voiced by angels at the ascension of Christ, for when He left this earth to go back to His Father the event left his followers gazing up into heaven at the awesome sight, and angels came to comfort their hearts:

> Ye men of Galilee, why stand ye gazing up into heaven? This same Jesus, which is taken up from you into heaven, shall so come in like manner as ye have seen him go into heaven (Acts 1:11).

It would be an almost impossible task to set down all the Scripture verses dealing with the Lord's return. An ancient scribe figured that one out of every 25 verses in the New Testament affirms His coming again. Any casual reader of the Bible would have no trouble in finding all the proof necessary to undergird his faith in the doctrine. Types and shadows of the glorious event are found in the Old Testament along with numerous prophecies among all the prophetic writings; and to this must be added the clear teachings of our Lord and of the apostles.

Where is the promise of His coming? It is written in the heart of God, who is not about to write off the planet Earth as a loss in His universe. He who has engraven Israel upon the palms of His hands, and who loves all members of the human race even in their rebellion, has planned to make this place the capital of the universe.

It is a long and complex plan devised by God himself. It includes the regathering of Israel from among the nations to the land of Palestine. It includes the restoring of moral order and the putting down of all rebellion. It includes the exaltation of His Son above every name in heaven or earth. It includes the final imprisonment forever of all willful rebels against His plans. His purpose in the world is to have a race of men living in quietness and peace, without sin, worshiping Him willingly and lovingly. And when that plan finds its culmination, it can be said:

> Behold, the tabernacle of God is with men, and he will dwell with them, and they shall be his people, and God himself shall be with them, and be their God. And God shall wipe away all tears from their eyes; and there shall be no more death, neither sorrow, nor crying, neither shall there be any more pain: for the former things are passed away (Revelation 21:3, 4).

3 The Cloud of His Appearing

> Behold, he cometh with clouds; and every eye shall see him, and they also which pierced him: and all kindreds of the earth shall wail because of him. Even so, Amen (Revelation 1:7).

The coming of the Lord shall be with clouds. Such is indicated by many Scriptures having to do with His coming to reign upon this earth. Just as the clouds herald a change in the climate in the natural realm, so the clouds of His coming herald a tremendous change of climate in the moral realm, for mighty changes shall be wrought upon the earth when Jesus comes again.

"A cloud received him out of their sight," said the writer of Acts 1:9, and the angels said, "He shall so come in like manner as ye have seen him go."

Dr. J. A. Seiss, in his sermon on the Second Coming, said:

> Few believe this, and still fewer lay it to heart. Many sneer at the very idea, and would fain laugh down the people who are so simple as to entertain it. But it is nevertheless the immutable truth of God, predicted by His prophets, promised by Christ himself, confirmed by the testimony of angels, pro-

claimed by the apostles, believed by all the early Christians, acknowledged in all the church creeds, sung about in all the church liturgies, and so essentially wrought into the very life and substance of Christianity, that without it there is no Christianity, except a few maimed and mutilated relics too powerless to be worth the trouble or expense of preservation.

The Scriptures teach that Jesus Christ who ascended from Mt. Olivet before the wondering gaze of His disciples shall come from heaven and stand again on that very summit from which He went up. "With clouds" indicates the characteristics of majesty and glory, the awful pomp and splendor of Him "who maketh the clouds his chariot: who walketh upon the wings of the wind" (Psalm 104:3).

All who have ever lived, or shall live, shall be compelled to look upon Him. The dead shall be brought to life again and stand in His presence. The nation of Israel, which gave us the blessings of Christianity and then turned from their Messiah to live for centuries in their apostasy, shall see Him. The Gentile nations, largely living in rejection of Christ in spite of millions of Bibles and massive waves of evangelism and missionary activity, shall all give an account at the coming of the Lord.

John saw all this, and in simple words emphatically stated: "Every eye shall see him, and they also which pierced him; and all kindreds of the earth shall wail because of him."

Daniel the prophet, while working in the higher political brackets of Babylon, was given marvelous insight regarding world affairs. While he was in the position of first president of Persia, God gave him great understanding concerning the future, and he saw the coming of a succession of kingdoms that would keep the nation of Israel and the city of Jerusalem in subjugation. This long period of time would be known as the "times of the Gentiles." The period would end with the return of the Messiah to take possession of the throne of David, to restore the glory of the nation of Israel, and to make Jerusalem a praise in the earth. After the vision of the beasts which typified the unregenerate kingdoms of earth, Daniel said:

> I beheld till the thrones were cast down, and the Ancient of days did sit, whose garment was white as snow, and the hair of his head like the pure wool: his throne was like the fiery flame, and his wheels as burning fire. . . . I saw in the night visions, and, behold, one like the Son of man came *with the clouds of heaven,* and came to the Ancient of days, and they brought him near before him. And there was given him dominion, and glory, and a kingdom, that all people, nations, and languages, should serve him: his dominion is an everlasting dominion, which shall not pass away, and his kingdom that which shall not be destroyed (Daniel 7:9, 13,14).

The clouds of majesty and glory will dispel the many clouds that have brought havoc to the earth through the centuries. An era of righteousness shall be ushered in, and the nations shall learn war no more. People will not have to say, "Do you know the Lord?" for all shall know Him from the least unto the greatest (Jeremiah 31:34).

When Jesus was here in the flesh it was hard for the multitudes at large to grasp the fact that He was a unique person, different from every other person who ever walked the earth. They could not and did not know of His virgin birth, and so they asked, "Is not this the carpenter's son?" To the rulers and the learned it was unthinkable that a poverty-stricken town like Bethlehem could be the birthplace of a king, or that any good thing could come out of Nazareth. In short, there was little or nothing to commend the natural life of Jesus to the natural eye of man. When they looked upon His background, His life, and His general appearance there was no special beauty that they should desire Him. The eternal Word had become flesh and the eternal glory had become perfectly veiled under the garment of humanity. He was walking in a world He had made, and yet the world was oblivious to the fact that its Creator was in its midst, because of the perfect veiling accomplished in taking upon himself the form of man.

However, there were those occasions when, to the eye of faith, the eternal glory was made manifest in the words He uttered and in the acts He performed After He turned the water to wine at the wedding in Cana, and after amazing the guests by the sudden change in the general trend of events on that occasion, the Scriptures tell us, "This beginning of miracles . . . *manifested forth his glory;* and his disciples believed on him" (John 2:11). The power and glory that were His before the foundation of the world were made known by Him to bring joy to the hearts of men. Every miracle He performed constituted a showing forth of His divine credentials. He was a man; He was the God-man. He was the eternal Word clothed with flesh, and when His glory flashed forth in miraculous acts, "we beheld his glory, the glory of the only begotten of the Father, full of grace and truth" (John 1:14).

Along with the display of divine credentials in the mighty acts that Christ performed, and the display of glory on the Mount of Transfiguration, some of our Lord's utterances predicted a time of glory yet to come that would be worldwide in scope, and that would set forth His glory to the adoring wonder of angels and saints, and to the amazement of His enmies. One of these utterances is recorded in Mark 14. Standing before the chief priests at the trial of the Lord were several witnesses who were not able to agree in their testimony concerning Him. Suddenly the high priest stood up and directly challenged Jesus: "Art thou the Christ, the Son of the Blessed?" Jesus replied, "I am: and ye shall see the Son of man sitting on the right hand of power, and coming in the clouds of heaven" (vv. 61, 62).

This indicated His equality with God, and sounded like blasphemy to the high priest, for which Jesus was promptly sentenced to death. However, had they been men of faith, and had they known the Scriptures, they would have let their minds go back to the prophecy of Daniel, who said, "I saw in the night visions, and, behold, one like the Son of man came with the clouds of heaven" (Daniel 7:13).

When commenting on the visions of Daniel—that the kingdoms of earth are seen as a succession of wild beasts until the Lord comes to rule—Myer Pearlman offered the following:

> Daniel, after watching the procession of wild beasts, must have asked in distress, "Lord, does the future belong to nations who practice violence and oppression? Does one have to be hard and cruel to succeed in this world? Does might make right? Does the future belong to the terrible beast who will make war against God and His people?" And God seemed to say, "Daniel, get your eyes off the wild beasts and look up." And Daniel looked, and instead of wild beasts he saw the Son of Man coming in the heavens. Cruel beasts and a compassionate Man—there is the contrast. There is no future for those beasts, for nations that choose injustice and violence as their guiding spirit. Get your eyes on the Son of man in glory. The future belongs to Him.

It is necessary that Jesus come to this earth again. Man in his rejection of God has made a mess of things. His depraved heart sinks lower and lower into the unpleasantness of sin. He cannot stop making war on his fellowman, for wars are born out of the lusts of his degenerate heart. Everything man puts his hand to he ruins. His own vaunted wisdom is born out of imperfect knowledge, and all his grandiose schemes for the future lead down blind alleys. Those who feel they have the answers to the world's problems have run themselves into an endless circle of councils, treaties, conferences, leagues, etc., none of which have continued long or brought about the desired results. If man were to be allowed to continue indefinitely in his sinful condition, the entire planet would become like hell itself. It is imperative that Jesus come again, for in Him are all the treasures of wisdom and knowledge needed to guide man's affairs in the future.

Jesus must come again, or the life of faith for Christian people will forever remain without a culminating point—unfulfilled, unrealized, a continual walking through the night without ever seeing the Daystar. We have read about God in the Bible, and are intensely grateful for such a magnificent revelation. We have learned of His attributes of character, of His ways, of His mighty acts, of His covenants, of His plans and programs, but we shall forever lack something in our knowledge and understanding until the day we see Him in whom "dwelleth all the fulness of the Godhead bodily" (Colossians 2:9), and see Him in His exalted position as King of kings and Lord of lords—as perfect Man and perfect God. What a gloriour day God has in store for this world when all prophecies are fulfilled and the sinful career of this earth is forever past. Then shall come the conditions of heaven on earth, when "the tabernacle of God is with men, and he will dwell with them, and they shall be his people, and God himself shall be with them, and be their God" (Revelation 21:3).

Looking beyond these present centuries to the far distant future, the eminent F. B. Meyer posed the question, "Who knows but what earth is the seed-plot for the whole universe?" He felt that as long as earth continued its sinful career, man would be barred from setting up living conditions in other parts of the universe; but when the sinful career of earth is ended, man may be at liberty to explore the far-flung universe which the Creator has made, and earth could be the seed-plot from which other planets and galaxies will be populated. This infinite enterprise would continue through coming ages, bringing unending and ever-growing glory to the Creator of us all. Such may seem very imaginative, but God has set eternity in the heart of man, and the creature God made in His own image is destined for eternal priesthood and kingship while the cycles of eternity roll along.

Whatever the future holds, the coming of Jesus in the clouds of heaven is the key that will unlock the mystery. Friend, look up! The cloud of His appearing will soon be seen.

It may grow darker and darker in this world as men grope in their blindness, but for those who have caught a glimpse of God's program for the future, the Daystar is soon to appear. Let your faith soar upward. Let out the rein on your hopes and aspirations. Never lose sight of the fact that "all the promises of God in him are yea, and in him Amen, unto the glory of God by us" (2 Corinthians 1:20). He is coming again, and the clouds of glory will bring an end—the final end—to misgivings, doubts, fears, and the trials of faith that God's children have had in this life.

On the flyleaf of a library book were found the

following lines, penned by an ardent student of the Bible:

> I am standing just now on the threshold
> Of a land that is fairer than day;
> I am hiding securely in Jesus,
> 'Til He speaks saying, "Up and away!"
>
> Then through outer space I will travel,
> With a speed the sound waves never knew,
> To the haven prepared for God's pilgrims
> Who have valiantly fought their way through.

4 Coming for His Church

The doctrine of the Rapture of the Church was a mystery revealed to Paul. It is not taught in the Old Testament, though it appears to be typified in the translation of Enoch before the outpouring of God's wrath at the time of the Flood; and it was only hinted at by our Lord when, after speaking about the troubles of the Tribulation period, He said, "Pray that ye may be accounted worthy to escape all these things, and to stand before the son of man."

When Paul introduced the subject to the Thessalonian church, it was with the words, "I would not have you to be ignorant, brethren . . ." (1 Thessalonians 4:13), and the subject was placed before the Corinthian church with the words, "Behold, I show you a mystery" (1 Corinthians 15:51).

The word *rapture* is not found in the Scriptures, but is taken from the Latin word *rapere* and the Greek word *harpadzo*, which means "caught up," meaning—to transport or take out of the world. It is the act of transporting or transferring a person from one place to another, as in the case of Enoch and Elijah. It is called in Scripture "the coming of the Lord" in the air (1 Thessalonians 4:15); "the resurrection of [from among] the dead" (Philippians 3:11); and "the blessed hope" (Titus 2:13). The Rapture and the Revelation should never be confused. They are two separate and, from every standpoint, distinct events.

The first coming was the first time Christ came to the earth to live and complete a special work of redemption.

The Second Coming is the second time He will come to earth to live and complete a special work in ridding the earth of all rebellion (1 Corinthians 15: 24-28; Revelation 19:11; Revelation 20:10).

The Rapture is purely a New Testament doctrine revealed for the first time to Paul (1 Corinthians 15:51).

Two key Scriptures that set forth the doctrine of the Rapture are the following:

> For the Lord himself shall descend from heaven with a shout, with the voice of the archangel, and with the trump of God: and the dead in Christ shall rise first: Then we which are alive and remain shall be caught up together with them in the clouds, to meet the Lord in the air, and so shall we ever be with the Lord (1 Thessalonians 4:16, 17).

> Behold I show you a mystery; We shall not all sleep, but we shall all be changed, in a moment, in the twinkling of an eye, at the last trump; for the trumpet shall sound, and the dead shall be raised incorruptible, and we shall be changed (1 Corinthians 15:51, 52).

By breaking the doctrine of the Rapture up into seven points, we may view it in this manner:

- Revelation: "This we say unto you by the word of the Lord . . ."
- Return: "For the Lord himself shall descend from heaven . . ."

- Resurrection: "And the dead in Christ shall rise first . . ."
- Rapture: "Then we which are alive and remain shall be caught up . . ."
- Reunion: "Together with them . . ."
- Reception: "To meet the Lord in the air . . ."
- Refreshment: "Wherefore comfort one another with these words."

The Rapture: for All Christians

There are those who believe this glorious event will happen for certain select saints who have reached a certain status in Christian living. Others believe the Church must go through the Tribulation; and still others have taught that the Church must go through the first half of that time of judgment.

It is not necessary to speculate on these things, for the Scriptures are very plain. A person becomes a Christian the moment he gives his life to Christ through repentance of sin and faith toward God. When the blood of Jesus cleanses a person from all sin, that person is a Christian. He may be an infant in spiritual things, not having yet learned much of the Word, or developed a prayer life, or had any experiences in God beyond conversion. Let us remember that maturity is a matter of development as we walk with the Lord and learn of His Word; but our standing before God as His child is settled once we have been converted to Christ. And the Scriptures teach that all who have died *in* Christ, and all who are living *in* Christ when the Rapture takes place, will be caught up to be with the Lord in the air. Not one of the trophies of His redeeming grace will be left behind.

This will be the glorious moment when that which had been sown in weakness shall be raised in power; and when that which had been sown in dishonor shall be raised in glory. With the rising of the righteous from the realms of the dead, an instantaneous change shall take place in the bodies of the living believers. "We shall not all sleep (or, be dead) but we shall all be changed, in a moment, in the twinkling of an eye, at the last trump; for the trumpet shall sound, and the dead shall be raised incorruptible, and we shall be changed."

More light is shed upon this glorious change in Philippians 3:20 (New International Version):

> For our citizenship is in heaven from whence also we look for the Saviour, the Lord Jesus Christ, who shall change our vile body, that it may be fashioned like unto his glorious body.

The American Standard Version says,

> . . . who shall fashion anew the body of our humiliation, that it may be conformed to the body of his glory.

This transformation in the bodies of the dead and the living saints at the coming of Christ is called by Paul "the redemption of our body" (Romans 8:23). This is the blessed hope.

There is nothing blessed about the Church's going into the Tribulation to observe the wrath of God upon a wicked world. Logic itself would dare to ask, "If the wrath of God fell upon a substitute for me at Calvary, and if I accepted that act, then why should the wrath of God fall upon me in the Tribulation?" Logic would also ask, "Why would God treat the last generation of Christian people during the Church Age any different than He treated all other generations since the Church began?" A careful study of several Scripture passages will convince the student that the Church is a special body in the world, and will be dealt with by the Lord in a special manner.

Robert Laidlaw, of Auckland, New Zealand, stated, "Teach the doctrine of the Lord's imminent coming, the hope and inspiration of the Early Church, and you send away the people of God lifted up, their hearts throbbing with joyous expectation: but teach that the Church will go through the Tribulation and you send Christians out in despondency and doubt, with no spontaneous Hallelujah in their hearts."

The reason why many Bible students have gone astray in this matter is that they have failed to distinguish between those passages in the Word that relate to the Rapture and those that relate to the Revelation: in other words, they have failed to see that the Scripture teaches most clearly that Christ will come *for* His saints, and that Christ will come *with* His saints, and that His coming for His saints must necessarily precede His coming with His saints.

The Rapture: Foreshadowed in the Old Testament

If the saints are going to have to go through the Tribulation it would be better for us to die than to live until Jesus comes. So terrible will be the storm of the Tribulation that it would be better to be sleeping beneath the sod, our spirits with the Lord in the glory awaiting the dawn of the resurrection morning, than to be living here on the earth. During the Tribulation men will seek death, and not be able to find it; they will desire to die and death will flee from them (Revelation 9:6).

It is important that we keep in mind that types simply illustrate or emphasize certain doctrines or teachings of the Word of God. They are designed to illustrate what in other places in the inspired Word is set forth in language that is so plain that he who runs may read.

It is clear from what our Lord said when He was here that the Flood in Noah's day may be regarded as a type of the Tribulation. It is clear also that the destruction that overtook the inhabitants of Sodom when God rained fire and brimstone from heaven and destroyed them all must be regarded as a type of the terrible destruction that will overtake multitudes of earth dwellers at the time of the end when the cup of earth's iniquity shall have become full. Jesus said:

> As it was in the days of Noah, so shall it be also in the days of the Son of man. They did eat, they drank, they married wives, they were given in marriage, until the day that Noah entered into the ark, and the flood came and destroyed them all. Likewise as it was in the days of Lot; they did eat, they drank, they bought, they sold, they planted, they builded; but the same day that Lot went out of Sodom it rained fire and brimstone from heaven and destroyed them all. Even thus shall it be in the day when the Son of man is revealed (Luke 17:26-30).

Enoch has always been regarded as a type of the saints who will go up at the time of the Rapture. When did he go up? It was before the Flood.

The fire and the brimstone did not fall upon the wicked city of Sodom until after righteous Lot had made his exit from the city. When Lot was told to go and urged to make haste in going, he begged that he might not be obliged to escape to the mountain lest some evil befall him.

> Behold, now, this city is near to flee unto and it is a little one: O, let me escape thither, . . . and my soul shall live (Genesis 19:20).

The angel to whom the appeal was made said,

> See, I have accepted thee concerning this thing also, that

I will not overthrow this city, for the which thou hast spoken. Haste thee, escape thither; for I cannot do anything till thou be come thither (Genesis 19:21, 22).

If the storm of divine wrath could not fall upon Sodom until righteous Lot had been delivered, how can the storm of divine wrath fall upon the earth until after the saints have been taken out? Did God have a greater interest in Lot than He has in the saints of this Church Age, who by virtue of having accepted Jesus Christ as their Saviour are linked with the living Christ who is the Head of the Church? The saints are the salt of the earth. Salt preserves. The Holy Spirit in the Church is the restraining influence that during this Church Age is preventing the mystery of iniquity from reaching its full and final development.

The mystery of iniquity doth already work; only he who now restraineth will restrain until he be taken out of the way. And then shall that lawless one be revealed, whom the Lord shall consume with the Spirit of his mouth, and shall destroy with the brightness of his coming, even him whose coming is after the working of Satan with all power and signs and lying wonders, and with all deceivableness of unrighteousness in them that perish; because they received not the love of the truth that they might be saved (2 Thessalonians 2:7-10).

The Rapture: an Imminent Event

In all generations of Church history the Christians have been exhorted to look for the return of the Lord for His people. They have never been told to look for the Antichrist, or for the Tribulation, or for Armageddon, or for any other personage or event—*only for the Lord*. No special sign or fulfilled prophecy was to precede the translation of the Church. This imminency was stressed in the teachings of our Lord:

And there shall be signs in the sun, and in the moon, and in the stars; and upon the earth distress of nations, with perplexity; the sea and the waves roaring; men's hearts failing them for fear, and for looking after those things which are coming on the earth: for the powers of heaven shall be shaken. And then shall they see the Son of man coming in a cloud with power and great glory. And when these things BEGIN TO COME TO PASS, then look up, and lift up your heads; for your redemption draweth nigh (Luke 21:25-28).

Again He said:

Take heed to yourselves, lest at any time your hearts be overcharged with surfeiting, and drunkenness, and cares of this life, and so that day come upon you unawares. For as a snare it shall come on all them that dwell on the face of the whole earth. Watch ye therefore, and pray always, that ye may be accounted worthy to escape all these things that shall come to pass, and to stand before the Son of man (Luke 21: 34-36).

Note the fact that it is not *after* these things shall have come to pass, but rather, "When ye see these things *begin* to come to pass," that we are exhorted to look up for our redemption draweth nigh.

The imminency of the Rapture is taught by Paul. The day of judgment talked about in the Revelation is called the "day of wrath and revelation of the righteous judgment of God" in Romans 2:5. In his sermon on Mars Hill, Paul said that God "hath appointed a day in the which he will judge the world in righteousness by that man whom he hath ordained; whereof he hath given assurance unto all men, in that he hath raised him from the dead" (Acts 17:31). Our Lord taught very definitely that believers are to have no part in that judgment. In John 5:22-24 we read, "For the Father judgeth no man, but hath committed all judgment unto the Son . . . He that heareth my word, and believeth on him that sent me, hath everlasting life, and shall not come into condemnation; but is passed from death unto life." The word rendered "condemnation" means *judgment,* and is so rendered in the A.S.V., where we are distinctly told that the believer "cometh not into judgment."

The imminency of the Rapture is taught in the letters to the churches in Revelation 2 and 3. You are no doubt familiar with the promise of our Lord to the angel of the church in Philadelphia:

> Because thou hast kept the word of my patience, I also will keep thee from the hour of temptation, which shall come upon all the world, to try them that dwell upon the earth. (Revelation 3:10).

We are told here what the object of the Tribulation will be—to try the earth dwellers. It is interesting to notice how often in the Revelation reference is made to them "that dwell upon the earth." It is a study in itself, and the reference is never to the saints, but always to sinners.

Let us not forget that the modernistic Laodicean period and the Philadelphian period with its open door of spiritual opportunities run along side by side. We are living in the Laodicean period, but we do not belong to Laodicea; we belong to Philadelphia if we are true born-again believers.

The promise is clear and definite. The Greek preposition here rendered "from" means "out of" or "out side of." It is *ek* in the Greek, and is rendered "out of" 165 times in the New Testament. It occurs in such places as Matthew 2:6, "*Out of* thee shall come a governor"; Matthew 2:15, "*Out of* Egypt have I called my son"; Matthew 7:5, "First cast out the beam *out of* thine own eye; and then shalt thou see clearly to cast out the mote *out of* thy brother's eye."

The meaning then of the promise is clear. It is a blessed assurance given by our Lord that the saints are not scheduled to go through the Tribulation.

> God commendeth his love toward us, in that, while we were yet sinners, Christ died for us. Much more than, being now justified by his blood, *we shall be saved from wrath through him* (Romans 5:8-10).

The Rapture Is the Blessed Hope

There is nothing blessed about anticipating the wrath to come. The blessedness of our hope consists of the fact that the Church is destined to be with the Lord before the wrath of God is poured out. A careful study of the Word will convince the student that the Church is a special body in the world, and will be dealt with by the Lord in a special manner.

In all messages of judgment upon this world it is significant that the Church is never seen. The chapters in the Book of Revelation dealing with judgment can be thoroughly searched, but the Church is not seen on the earth during this time of wrath, simply because the Church is not appointed unto wrath. Our judgment fell upon our substitute at Calvary. Jesus Christ took the thunderbolts of God's wrath against sin in His own body on the tree, and there is no condemnation upon those who have received Christ as their personal friend and substitute.

The Jewish nation has an appointment with God during the Tribulation, for the period is designated by the prophet Jeremiah as the time of Jacob's trouble. The nations of the world also have an appointment with the wrath of God during those years, culminating in Armageddon. But Christ bore the wrath of God for you and me, and took the full penalty of the Law for sin. How beautifully Paul words it to the Thessalonians:

> For God hath not appointed us to wrath, but to obtain salvation by our Lord Jesus Christ, who died for us, that, whether we wake or sleep, we should live together with him. Wherefore comfort yourselves together, and edify one another, even as also ye do (1 Thessalonians 5:9-11).

Not until the Tribulation is ended do you see the Church again in the glory with Christ, enjoying the

Marriage Supper of the Lamb, and coming with Him in glory at His second literal coming to the earth.

The Church is to watch for the return of Christ in the clouds of glory. The Christians of Thessalonica were "waiting for God's Son from heaven," and Titus 2:13 teaches us that if we deny ungodliness and worldly lusts, and if we live soberly, righteously, and godly in this present world, we should also look for "that blessed hope, and the glorious appearing of the great God and our Saviour Jesus Christ."

It is wonderful to note that wheresoever this doctrine surfaces in the Bible, there is the implied incentive to more holy living. D. L. Moody said, "I have felt like working three times as hard since I came to understand that my Lord is coming again."

The Church is to be judged and married between the Rapture and the Revelation of Christ to the world. It can be categorically stated that the Judgment Seat of Christ and the Marriage Supper of the Lamb are literal events, the first where the believers will receive rewards according to the deeds done in the body, and the second where the Church is forever joined to Christ to rule and reign with Him throughout coming ages.

The Church is to be removed before the Antichrist is revealed. Throughout this dispensation the Church is presented as the salt of the earth and the light of the world. Sinful forces cannot utterly overwhelm the earth so long as the Holy Spirit is in the Church and the Church is in this world. The presence of the body of true believers in Christ constitutes a savoring influence in this world that keeps a semblance of order. When the Church is lifted into the air—when the restraining influence is gone—when the work of the Holy

Spirit in the Church is through and the time for judgment is come, then shall that wicked one be revealed.

The Church is made up of ambassadors for Christ. God has scattered us among the nations of the world to beseech men and women to "be reconciled to God." But when God is about to pour out His wrath upon the nations of the world because of their rejection and rebellion, He will first call His ambassadors home to be with himself. Among the nations of the world, when war is about to break out, diplomatic relations are broken off, and important personages and citizens are called back to their mother countries. So, when the Church's work for this dispensation is finished, the voice of the archangel will sound, and the Lord shall utter His glorious shout, and the saints will go to be with Him—and He shall meet them in the air.

An interesting feature of the blessed hope is that it is timeless. Every generation has been encouraged to look for the event. Great major fulfillments precede the literal second coming of Christ, but no prophecy can be singled out as having a mandatory fulfillment before the Rapture. We are rather exhorted that at the very beginning of any prophetic fulfillments we are to look up, for our redemption will be drawing nigh.

The waiting period has seemed long to God's dear children, but I am certain that God is working on schedule. When Jesus was on earth He said He did not know when He would return, nor did the angels, but the Father in heaven knew.

The Church: a Special Body

The whole Church Age is parenthetical and comes between the 69th and 70th weeks mentioned in Daniel 9:24-27. The 70th week concerns "thy people (Israel) and thy holy city (Jerusalem)" just as did the first 69 weeks. The purpose is to deal with Israel during this period to break them and bring them to repentance. There is no reason why the New Testament saints should go through this, but the period is necessary for Israel, to finish the six features of Daniel 9:24. Thus Israel is identified in chapters 4 through 19 of the Revelation for the purpose of fulfilling those features; namely, "to finish the transgression, and to make an end of sins, and to make reconciliation for iniquity, and to bring in everlasting righteousness, and to seal up the vision and prophecy, and to anoint the Most Holy" (Daniel 9:24).

The enthroned elders are representatives of the raptured saints and are always seen in heaven after their mention in Revelation 4:1. The crowns, white raiment, their distinction from angels throughout, the word "elders," and other identifications of humanity prove them to be redeemed human beings.

An individual is recognized and identified by his features and characteristics. A body of individuals is also identified by its peculiarities. So in this case, if the Church is on earth during the fulfillment of Revelation 4 through 19 we must see its earmarks; but such are not found. On the other hand, evidence of Israel is seen everywhere in the Revelation after chapter 4 and verse 1, a fact more striking since Israel is not once mentioned in chapters 1 through 3 where the Church is mentioned 19 times. The Jewish character of the Book of Revelation is evidenced by about 285 references to Israel such as the lamb, lion of Judah, offspring of David, 144,000 Jews, seals, trumpets, vials, altar and priestly ministry, horns of the altar, the prophets, temple, temple court, holy city, olive trees, ark of the covenant, woman and manchild, Michael, remnant, Armageddon, and scores of other references that are distinctively Jewish and were never mentioned in connection with the Church.

It may be stated then, in summary, that the purpose of the Rapture is that Christ might receive the saints unto himself in the air, and take them to heaven where they will be presented before God the Father to be forever with Him. It is to resurrect the dead "in Christ" from among the wicked dead and to change the bodies of all the saints to immortality. It is to make the saints "whole" in body, soul, and spirit, and to receive the fruits of the early and latter rain of the Holy Spirit in this dispensation. It is to cause the saints to escape the Tribulation and to stand before the Son of man. It is to remove the Hinderer of lawlessness, and to permit the revelation of the Antichrist.

No wonder that our God has urged all true believers to be without spot or wrinkle and without blemish. The event is for His people who have been cleansed by the blood of Jesus Christ and who are found in the way of truth and holiness.

5 Coming to Judge the World

And the kings of the earth, and the great men, and the rich men, and the chief captains, and the mighty men, and every bondman, and every free man, hid themselves in the dens and in the rocks of the mountains; and said to the mountains and rocks, Fall on us, and hide us from the face of him that sitteth on the throne, and from the wrath of the Lamb: for the great day of his wrath is come; and who shall be able to stand? (Revelation 6:15-17)

There are many paradoxes in the Bible, not the least of which is the fact that the Lamb of God, that One who opened not His mouth when accused by His countrymen, and who was led as a sheep to the slaughter, shall one day exercise such wrath as to make the mightiest of earth tremble and wish for death rather than face Him.

God must judge the earth because of its wickedness. Looking back over the pages of human history, we see a continuous and unbroken record of rebellion against righteousness. Civilization after civilization and nation after nation have walked in the way of godlessness and rebellion, and men in all walks of life are anticipating some visitation of God's wrath on earth because of iniquity. People are prone to ask, "Where will it all end?' Others in their willful ignorance and blindness refuse to acknowledge that anything is different, but insist that all things continue as they were for centuries past. Still others sense an impending breakdown of the present social, political, and finacial order, but do not know where to turn for guidance and counsel. The statesmen are at their wits' end. The modernistic and liberal churches who have refused God's Word have no other answer beyond their social ethics and psychological approach to the problems. The military men hope for peace and prepare for war. The politicians sit at their treaty tables trying to find a way out of the international delemma. They fawn over one another, drink cocktails together, sign documents, smile, bow low to dignitaries, but God gives His appraisal of all such: "The words of his mouth were smoother than butter, but war was in his heart" (Psalm 55:21).

When Jesus spoke of "distress among nations, with perplexity" (Luke 21:25), He used a word, *aporia*, which means "no way out, a state of quandary." The world's finest statesmen have never found the bridge that spans the gulf between war and perpetual peace. They are constantly beset by problems, new and old, stemming from the fallen nature of humanity, and no sooner is one problem resolved than another crops up in its place. So God has determined to bring the nations of the world to a place of judgment, and the Judge shall be none other than the Lamb of God in His role as the lion of the tribe of Judah.

> For the Father judgeth no man, but hath committed all judgment unto the Son (John 5:22).

> For as the Father hath life in himself; so hath he given to

the Son to have life in himself; and hath given him authority to execute judgment also, because he is the Son of man (John 5:26, 27).

The theology of the seven-years Tribulation is set forth in the prophecies of Daniel. It will be the 70th week (of years) set apart by God for special dealings with Israel and the city of Jerusalem.

Seventy weeks are determined upon thy people and upon thy holy city . . . (Daniel 9:24).

The first 69 weeks (483 years) are said to have begun with "the commandment to restore and to build Jerusalem," and they were to end with the cutting off of the Messiah.

A long parenthesis which we know as the Dispensation of Grace, or the Church Age, was to follow before the events of the 70th week could take place. This was not seen by Daniel, but was taught by our Lord. He said He would build His Church. He told the disciples not to worry about the times or the seasons which the Father had in His own power. They were to bring the gospel to the ends of the earth, and were to look for the Church to be caught up to be with the Lord. They were to watch and pray always. The time of God's wrath taught by so many of the prophets appeared to be held in abeyance. Nevertheless, in His magnificent Olivet discourse, Jesus said:

And this gospel of the kingdom shall be preached in all the world for a witness unto all nations; and then shall the end come (Matthew 24:14).

Immediately following that statement He warned the people of Israel about the holocaust to come:

For then shall be great tribulation, such as was not since the beginning of the world to this time, no, nor ever shall be (v. 21).

The word *tribulation* in its simplest form has been applied to the trials and sufferings the Church has always endured by being God's people on a pilgrimage through an alien and wicked world. But in the prophetic sense it always refers to a time of unprecedented judgment and wrath of God upon the earth. Jeremiah labeled it, "the time of Jacob's trouble" (30:7). A very extensive description of this period is in Zephaniah 1:14-18:

> The great day of the Lord is near, it is near, and hasteth greatly, even the voice of the day of the Lord: the mighty man shall cry there bitterly. That day is a day of wrath, a day of trouble and distress, a day of wasteness and desolation, a day of darkness and gloominess, a day of clouds and thick darkness, a day of the trumpet and alarm against the fenced cities, and against the high towers.
>
> And I will bring distress upon men, that they shall walk like blind men, because they have sinned against the Lord: and their blood shall be poured out as dust, and their flesh as the dung. Neither their silver nor their gold shall be able to deliver them in the day of the Lord's wrath; but the whole land shall be devoured by the fire of his jealousy: for he shall make even a speedy riddance of all them that dwell in the land.

A day of wrath . . . a day of trouble . . . distress . . . wasteness . . . desolation . . . gloominess . . . clouds and darkness . . . a day of alarm . . . death. It is not a pretty picture, but you may check all the references to the Tribulation, and there is a notable absence of mercy and comfort to mitigate the suffering, except it be the shortening of the time. It will be the worst period in all the annals of human history, and Jesus said the days would have to be shortened or no flesh would be saved on the earth. Remember that the Church, the salt of the earth, will be gone, and corruption and sin will reach its zenith. The violence that filled the earth in the days of Noah will be repeated; and the immorality that characterized Sodom and Gomorrah will be rampant throughout the earth.

John's Vision on Patmos

The apostle John, in writing about the details of the Tribulation, refers to "the winepress of the wrath of God" (Revelation 14:10-19); "vials full of the wrath of God" (15:7; 16:1); "all nations shall taste of the cup of the wine of his wrath" (16:19).

John portrays the wrath and judgment to be so intense that people of all walks of life will pray to the rocks and mountains to hide them from the wrath of God. Kings of earth, to whom the homage of millions has been given, will have no power then. Great men—men of science, men of letters, men of great influence—will be as nothing before these judgments. Rich men will not have enough riches to shield themselves or isolate themselves from the horrors to come. Chief captains and mighty men will not have enough legions or armaments to withstand the desolations. How puny man is before the wrath of God!

> Fall on us, and hide us from the face of him that sitteth on the throne, and from the wrath of the Lamb; for the great day of his wrath is come, and who shall be able to stand? (Revelation 6:16, 17).

Here, then, is a mighty volume of prayer—but no repentance. They are not sorry for their sins, but only sorry they got caught.

The beginning of this time of trouble was seen by John in his vision of the horsemen. First, a white horse and rider began to roam the earth, a reference to a great false peace movement bringing the world under the authority of a world ruler. Peace movements, brought about by the efforts of men, have always failed. There was a period of only about 20 years between World Wars I and II, in spite of the efforts of the League of Nations; and the past several years have been filled with wars in Korea, Veitnam, Nigeria, Bangladesh, Israel, together with the internal problems of many countries, in spite of the efforts of the United Nations.

"There is no peace, saith the Lord, unto the wicked" (Isaiah 48:22). The nations are like the troubled sea casting up its mire and dirt. Peace is their desire, but it always eludes their grasp. It is interesting to hear the statesmen speak of the need for world government, with a strong man at its head, to bring order out of the chaos. Paul-Henri Spaak, first Belgian ambassador to the United Nations, pleaded before that body for a strong man to step forth, if one were available, to solve the dilemma of our time. Most nations realize the need for a unified strategy, but few are willing to yield their power to a central agency. The attitude of self-will and self-dependence is just as ingrained in human nature now as it was when they cried out, "We will not have this man to rule over us."

The second horse and rider in John's vision was red, the symbol of war, and power was given to take peace from the earth "that they should kill one another" (Revelation 6:4). Perhaps none of us can really appreciate the restraining power that is exercised by the Holy Spirit and the presence of the Church on the earth. Were it not for this salt, this light, this restraining power, all hell would break loose upon the earth. Even with the Church present, the forces of evil are powerful, crime increases, and there is a disregard for human life; but when the Church is caught up, and the restraining power is lifted, the lusts and hatreds of men will break out in bloodshed such as earth has never known.

The third horse and rider in John's vision was black, the symbol of famine, poverty, and want. In just the past two or three years the prices of foodstuffs have soared until many products are beyond the reach of the average buyer. The increase of population all over the earth, drought conditions, inflation, and other causes have brought about a scarcity of many commodities that were once considered basic to daily living. It is said that India has a famine every five years. China has been desolated more than once by food shortages, and in 1974 alone the famine south of the Sahara took the lives of tens of thousands of people. Jeremiah, in his Lamentations, spoke of the famine in Jerusalem when that city was besieged in his day, when faces gathered blackness, and women ate their own children, and records show that men, who formerly were friends, fought like beasts over a crust of bread. Imagine scenes like that all over the earth during the Tribulation sorrows.

The fourth horse and rider was pale in color, the symbol of death.

> And power was given unto them over the fourth part of the earth, to kill with sword, and with hunger, and with death, and with the beasts of the earth (Revelation 6:8).

Earth's population at the present time is in excess of three billion. Imagine 750 million people dying violent deaths in the course of seven years or less. Imagine the tears, the suffering, the agony, the heartbreak, the graves; and yet there is no repentance on the part of humanity.

Trumpet Judgments

A catalog of all the events of the Tribulation would make a lengthy book in itself, but, in brief, John's vision heralded further sufferings in the sounding of the trumpets:

A trumpet sounds, and hail and fire mingled with blood destroy the third part of grass and trees (Revelation 8:7).

Another trumpet sounds, and the third part of the sea becomes like blood (v. 8).

Another trumpet sounds, and the rivers and fountains are affected, "and the third part of the waters became wormwood; and many men died of the waters, because they were made bitter" (v. 11).

Another trumpet sounds, and a third of the heavenly bodies are darkened, "so as the third part of them was darkened, and the day shone not for a third part of it, and the night likewise" (v. 12).

Another trumpet sounds, and the bottomless pit is opened and a demon horde is let loose over the face of the earth, having power like scorpions to torment men for five months.

> And in those days shall men seek death, and shall not find it; and shall desire to die, and death shall flee from them (Revelation 9:6).

Another trumpet sounds, and an army of 200 million destroys a third of earth's population (Revelation 9: 13-21).

Vials of Wrath

With nothing in past history to use as a comparison, it is next to impossible for our minds to comprehend the staggering implications of the foregoing judgments that will come, and yet, according to John, there were yet more frightful plagues and judgments to follow. In his vision of horrors he saw angels ready "to pour out vials of the wrath of God upon the earth."

The first angel poured out his vial upon the earth, "and there fell a noisome and grievous sore upon the men which had the mark of the beast, and upon them which worshipped his image" (Revelation 16:2). Such a plague fell upon Egypt in the days of Moses, a grievous ulcerated condition for which the Bible gives no time limit, and which, in this case, is limited to those who have willingly followed the Antichrist and taken his mark of allegiance.

The second angel poured out his vial upon the sea, "and it became as the blood of a dead man: and every living soul died in the sea" (16:3). Because these plagues have to do specifically with those who have followed the Antichrist, many believe the sea mentioned here is the Mediterranean, around which much of the Antichrist's kingdom is found.

The third angel poured out his vial upon the rivers and fountains of waters, "and they became blood." There is every reason to believe that this plague is literal, for such a plague was one that fell upon Egypt (Exodus 7:19-24). Lest someone should point an accusing finger at God for pouring out such wrath and fearsome judgments, an angel stepped forward in the vision to cry out,

> Thou art righteous, O Lord, which art, and wast, and shalt be, because thou hast judged thus. For they have shed the blood of saints and prophets, and thou hast given them blood to drink, for they are worthy (Revelation 16:5, 6).

Another angel stepped forward to confirm what had just been uttered and declared,

> Even so, Lord God Almighty, true and righteous are thy judgments (v. 7).

A fourth angel poured out his vial of wrath upon the sun,

> . . . and power was given unto him to scorch men with fire. And men were scorched with great heat, and blasphemed the name of God, which hath power over these plagues: and they repented not to give him glory (vv. 8, 9).

It was David who said that the heavens were the work of the hands of the Lord, and God's perfect control over the heavenly bodies was seen in the days of Joshua when the sun stood still in Gibeon and the moon in the valley of Ajalon while Joshua's army was engaged in battle. All nature responds to the commands of God. The treasure of the snow and hail are His. History in filled with incidents where God used the forces of nature to see that His plans were fulfilled, such as the unseasonable fog at Dunkirk that sheltered the British troops while they were being evacuated, and the bitter cold and deep snow that turned the forces of Napoleon back from Moscow. Men pride themselves in developing explosives and awesome powers in their arsenals, but the forces of nature, when unleashed, make men's efforts look puny by comparison.

Another angel poured out his vial of wrath upon the kingdom of the Antichrist, plunging it into darkness where men gnawed their tongues for pain and yet continued to blaspheme God. The Egyptian plague (Exodus 10) was such a darkness as could be felt, in which no one arose from his place until the plague lifted. This plague is stated to be upon "the kingdom of the Antichrist," showing its limitation to the area of his kingdom within the boundaries of the Roman Empire as it will then be revised.

A sixth angel poured out his vial of wrath upon the great river Euphrates, and that river, which has flowed since God made the garden of Eden, is dried up in this plague "that the way of the kings of the East might be prepared." The mighty Euphrates for centuries has been considered one of the major boundary lines between the Middle East and the Far East. It flowed out of Eden, survived the flood of Noah, and constituted one of nature's chief contributions to the farmland of the Fertile Crescent.

A hundred miles east of Aleppo at a place known as Tabqa, in Syria, a new dam is being erected at the cost of $400 million. The construction will displace 70,000 people, but the new dam and resulting benefits will make the northern half of Syria one of the most productive areas in the world. It will aid in the irrigation of more than 1.5 million acres of land and produce 2.5 billion kilowatt hours of electricity per year (three times the current Syrian production).

All of that looks good for Syria and will no doubt bring work, food, and prosperity to many in that part of the world. However, it is interesting to note that when many prophecies come to pass, they do so out of what seems to be a natural sequence of events so that people do not realize that a prophetic event has taken place. Even so, it would be easy with a massive dam high up in the Euphrates riverbed to close off the waters moving downstream and literally dry up the river. God could dry it up by His word, or by allowing an earthquake to divert the waters. But with the dam in Syria the possibilities are there for the stopping of the river through a series of natural events and thus bring the prophecy to pass, and God says the river shall be dried up "in the last days" to take away the main obstacle separating the armies of the Far East from coming into the Middle East.

When the seventh angel pours out his vial of wrath upon the earth, the result is the greatest earthquake of all time, "a great earthquake, such as was not since men were upon the earth, so mighty an earthquake, and so great" (Revelation 16:18). Jerusalem shall be separated by this quake into three parts, and the cities of the nations will fall. What carnage! What destruction! We have heard of small cities being devastated by earthquakes, but imagine the major cities of the nations of the world with their skyscrapers, their massive auditoriums, their high-rise apartments tumbling down in a mass of debris as the crust of the earth heaves and buckles under this vial of the wrath of God. Coupled with this awesome event will be a "great hail out of heaven, every stone about the weight of a talent [*talanton:* about 114 pounds]: and men blasphemed God because of the plague of the hail, for the plague thereof was exceeding great" (Revelation 16:17-21).

You may ask why? Why is God going to judge the world? How could a God, whose name is love, put such terrors upon men?

If you are asking that, it is because you have no true concept of the holiness of God and the enormity of sin. We have so little concept of the unholiness of man. We understand so little of God's attitude toward rebellion and rebellious people. We cannot comprehend such sins as would nail the fairest flower of heaven to a cross, and give Him vinegar to drink, and gamble away His garments with callous indifference. Before He brings the glorious millennial reign into being with His Son on the Throne, God must judge the world and bring mankind to face the fact of man's total depravity, and of God's infinite holiness, and what He requires to have true peace on earth.

God's Purposes in the Tribulation

In the judgments to come God has a purpose in relation to Israel. Through them the promised redemption was to bless the world. They had been given a God-ordained priesthood and sacrifices. They had been given the Law and the Prophets. They had been given covenants and promises that were to find their highest fulfillment whenever the Messiah came and was received by the nation; but when He came they rejected Him. They had watched with interest the development of His life, and had noted His miracles and listened to His words. But when He told them they could have no part in Him unless they repented of their sins, they were offended and said, "We have Moses and the prophets." Jesus was despised and rejected, and finally crucified by the very people He came to save. Their sin was not one of ignorance, but willful rejection.

In A.D. 70 the nation of Israel was dispersed, and the Christian era has found them scattered among all the countries of the world. However, Ezekiel (ch. 20) shows God's purpose for Israel in the Tribulation as causing them to pass under the rod of judgment, to purge out the rebels, and to leave a believing remnant with which to begin the glorious Kingdom.

> For in mine holy mountain, in the mountain of the height of Israel, saith the Lord God, there shall all the house of Israel, all of them in the land, serve me: there will I accept them, and there will I require your offerings, and the firstfruits of your oblations, with all your holy things. I will accept you with your sweet savor, when I bring you out from the people, and gather you out of the countries wherein ye have been scattered; and I will be sanctified in you before the heathen. And ye shall know that I am the Lord, when I shall bring you into the land of Israel, into the country for the which I lifted up mine hand to give it to your fathers. And there shall ye remember your ways, and all your doings, wherein ye have been defiled; and ye shall loathe yourselves in your own sight for all your evils that ye have committed (Ezekiel 20:40-43).

There is much in that prophecy yet to be fulfilled, but since World War II we have seen the gradual homecoming of Israel. In 1948 enough of them were in the land to declare themselves a nation and to begin political rapport with the other nations of the world. The regathering is going on. The land that has been idle for centuries can hold millions more, and approximately 13 million Jews are still scattered throughout other countries.

Another purpose of God in the Tribulation is in relation to the Gentile nations. All nations that have oppressed Israel will be special targets of the wrath of God. The Covenant God made with Abraham is still in effect, "Them that curse thee, I will curse." It is a most wonderful thing to be blest of God, and an awful thing to be cursed.

It is indeed strange to note the waves of anti-Semitism that have come from many countries. Israel has been made a proverb and a byword wherever found among the Gentiles. Though they have given the world great musicians, great scientists, great actors, and great statesmen, yet as an ethnic group they have been bemeaned and slandered more than any other on earth. God takes note of all this. God saw the "ultimate solution" imposed upon the Jews by Adolph Hitler, when the determination was made to blot every Jew out of existence, and Germany fell in turn under the bombs of the Allied armies. God also sees the attitude of godless communism against the Jew; but the armies of Meshech and Tubal shall be obliterated on the very mountains of Israel (Ezekiel 39, 40).

On the other hand, there have been nations that have stood side by side with Israel in their troubles, and God takes note of this. Who knows what the future holds for those nations that have befriended the Covenant people? God is debtor to no man—nor to any nation.

A third purpose of God in the Tribulation is to reveal the program of Satan in its true character, and to permit Lucifer's system to come to its logical end. Satan has always had a desire to rule a kingdom and to be worshiped by men. During Christ's temptation in the wilderness he paraded the kingdoms of the world before Jesus and said they had been delivered to him, and that Christ could have them if He would bow down to Satan. The great adversary has never wanted to recognize the true authority of God since the original rebellion in the heavens. But his system is a lawless one, and the logical end of all lawlessness is judgment, futility, and emptiness.

In spite of all the sin we see in the world, it is only a small part of what sinful hearts are capable of doing but cannot because of the restraining influence in the world. During the coming judgments this restraint will be lifted, and the full and true character of evil and rebellion will be manifest. God will let people have their own way on the earth. The lawless one will be revealed who opposeth and exalteth himself above all that is called God.

Friend, I am not looking for the Tribulation, but it is good to have information concerning the times to come so that we might warn others. Ours is a blessed hope offered to all who turn to Jesus Christ and make Him their friend and Saviour. We have His promise that He has delivered us from the wrath to come.

6 Coming as King of the Jews

And sitting down they watched him there: and set up over his head his accusation written, THIS IS JESUS THE KING OF THE JEWS (Matthew 27:36, 37).

For long years after Israel was brought out of Egypt's bondage the people had no king over them but God. His presence shining from the ark of the covenant in the Holy of Holies was sufficient. Appointed captains over hundreds, and over fifties, and over tens in the days of the wilderness wanderings were followed by judges in the land of Canaan. The prophet Samuel was the last (and probably the greatest) of the judges over the Israelites, but when he was old he appointed his sons to take his place. Samuel himself had been a very godly man, but his sons walked not in his ways; they turned aside after money, and took bribes, and perverted judgment. The people of the land chafed under such leadership, and, coming to the aged Samuel, they said, "Behold, thou art old, and thy sons walk not in thy ways: now make us a king to judge us like all the nations" (1 Samuel 8:5).

It was never God's intention that Israel should have any king but the Messiah. Their desire to have an earthly king was tantamount to a rejection of God's rulership over them. They wanted to be like other nations. Knowing what tyranny an earthly king can exercise over a nation, God told Samuel to make the people aware of the problems involved in having a man like themselves to take the reins of leadership and rule them. With a strong voice of protest Samuel said to the people:

> This will be the manner of the king that shall reign over you: He will take your sons, and appoint them for himself, for his chariots, and to be his horsemen; and some shall run before his chariots. And he will appoint him captains over thousands, and captains over fifties; and will set them to ear his ground and to reap his harvest, and to make his instruments of war, and instruments of his chariots. And he will take your daughters to be confectionaries, and to be cooks, and to be bakers. And he will take your fields, and your vineyards, and your olive-yards, even the best of them, and give them to his servants. And he will take the tenth of your seed, and of your vineyards, and give to his officers, and to his servants. And he will take your menservants, and your maidservants, and your goodliest young men, and your asses, and put them to work. He will take the tenth of your sheep; and ye shall be his servants. And ye shall cry out in that day because of your king which ye shall have chosen you; and the Lord will not hear you in that day (1 Samuel 8:11-18).

However, the people would not listen to Samuel, but said, "We will have a king over us; that we also may be like all the nations" (v. 19).

From the days of Samuel, who anointed Saul as Israel's first king, to A.D. 70, when the Roman legions of Titus besieged and destroyed Jerusalem, Israel either had a king of their own, or were in captivity under the heel of some Gentile king. Some of their kings sought the welfare of the nation, and the nation prospered under David and Solomon. The people were greatly helped in the days of the godly Josiah.

But kings like Ammon and Manasseh led the people into the grossest forms of idolatry and drained the resources of the nation for their own affluence and pleasure. The idolatry of Israel, even in the face of the preachings of Jeremiah, was such that the nation was invaded and went into captivity under Babylon for 70 years. This rulership by a Gentile nation was followed by the authority of the Medes and Persians, then of the Greeks, and then the brutal power of Rome. Oh, how the people groveled under the iron heel of their oppressors. They had wanted God in their times of need, but when things were going smoothly they wanted to be like the nations round about.

The Promised Messiah

Throughout the Old Testament two types of promises concerning the Messiah are found, and every promise concerning the Messiah in any form of His ministry falls into one of these two categories, for they speak either of His humiliation or of His exaltation. If the Israelites had read their Scriptures carefully they would have known that their Messiah had a dual ministry: first to come as a sacrifice for the sins of the whole world, and then to rule and to reign. The 53rd chapter of Isaiah gives a detailed account of the sufferings of the Messiah. Several of the psalms of David speak of incidents in His life as the sin-bearer. But Israel was not interested in a suffering Messiah. They wanted a king who would deliver them from the surrounding nations and make Israel the leader in the world—who would restore the temple, and bring affluence to the people.

When Jesus was first introduced to the people it was not as a king, but in His role of humiliation. John declared, "Behold the Lamb of God, which taketh away the sin of the world" (John 1:29). When the people knew Him better they were sure that He would make a great Messiah. He could feed the multitude with a little food, turn water into wine, control the stormy elements, rebuke the haughty, love the children, speak with authority, heal the sick, raise the dead—there really was nothing He could not do. But they found they could not manipulate Him.

His first goal was to suffer and die for the sins of the world before giving any consideration to reigning upon a throne; to this goal He set His face like a flint, and none could deter Him. His third year of ministry is often called "the year of rejection," for many of His closest followers left Him when He began to speak of going to a cross and dying. He had always seemed to be alienated from the high priests and rulers of the nation, who misjudged His motives and were afraid of their own positions. His holy life was a rebuke to their way of life. His doctrine had the ring of authority, while theirs was filled with uncertainty. In those final hours when He stood before Pilate they accused Him of insurrection against the government, since he claimed to be a king, and they cried, "We have no king but Caesar!" And they accused Him of blasphemy because He claimed to be the Son of God who should come in the clouds of heaven with power and great glory.

It was a sad spectacle. The hands that made the worlds held a reed scepter. The head that contained the knowledge and wisdom of the ages wore a crown of thorns. The body that had ministered to countless thousands wore a purple robe in mockery. The face that had shown compassion and understanding to the bereaved and needy now dripped with blood and with the spittle of uncouth men. Before the day was through, the hands and feet that brought the mercies of heaven into this world of corruption were nailed to a cross, and over His head was placed a sign that read, "This is Jesus, the King of the Jews."

While walking to His execution He paused to speak to a group of mourning women: "Daughters of Jerusalem, weep not for me, but weep for yourselves, and for your children" (Luke 23:28).

Yes, the prophecies concerning the humiliation of the Messiah had to come to pass. Jesus confirmed this to the disciples on the road to Emmaus after His resurrection when He said to them, "Ought not Christ to have suffered these things?" But He referred to that other body of prophecy concerning the exaltation of the Messiah when He added, "and to enter into His glory?"

No wonder the hearts of these disciples burned with a new understanding as Jesus unfolded to them both sides of the ministry of the Messiah.

"Until Shiloh Comes"

A most interesting prophecy was pronounced by the patriarch Jacob upon his son Judah. Jacob had reached the ripe age of 147 years. Knowing that he was about to die, he called all his sons around his bed "that I may tell you that which shall befall you in the last days" (Genesis 49:1). Beginning with Reuben, the old man laid his hands upon them each in turn and prophesied concerning the future of each tribe. Upon the head of Judah he pronounced a most remarkable prophecy. To paraphrase the predictions, Judah was to be praised by his brethren and take dominion over his enemies; the tribe of Judah was to be as a lion among the tribes, and hold the scepter of lawgiver.

From this tribe Shiloh was to come, and unto him would be the gathering of the people.

Shiloh in the Old Testament is the equivalent of Messiah in the New Testament. Inasmuch as Jacob was predicting that which would come to pass in the last days, the picture is plain that the Messiah, who should come from the tribe of Judah would rule all Israel. This was confirmed by the angel Gabriel when he told Mary, "He shall be great, and shall be called the Son of the Highest: and the Lord God shall give unto him the throne of his father David, and he shall reign over the house of Jacob for ever" (Luke 1:32, 33).

The people of Israel have been in no position to establish a government of their own during the past several centuries. Scarcely any have lived in Palestine, the covenant land; indeed, the very purpose behind the Dispersion was to scatter them to be subject to Gentile authority. Because of their innate drive and ingenuity many of them have greatly prospered. From them have come great scientists, mathematicians, showmen, musicians, and some great political leaders. Jonas Salk, Madame Curie, Bernard Baruch, Leonard Bernstein, Billy Rose, Benjamin Disraeli, Albert Einstein, Henry Kissinger have all become household names with respect to their own particular field of endeavor. These and many others have achieved eminence in spite of persecution. But the fact remains that Israel has been a scattered people under Gentile dominion.

It will not always be so. Israel wants a king. The people have been promised a king in their sacred writings, and it is highly significant that when in 1948 they became a nation again, they refrained from setting up a monarchy and chose instead a parliamentary form of government, reserving the throne of David for the only rightful heir to that throne—the coming Messiah.

The Reconciliation

Nearly all of the great events in the life of the Messiah were typified in the Old Testament; that is, some event in the Old Testament prefigures an event in the life of Christ. A most dramatic moment is coming when the Man who went to Calvary and had His hands and feet pierced by cruel nails will come face to face with the nation that rejected Him; and this event is prefigured by the account of Joseph's reunion with his brethren.

Joseph had dreamed of a day when the sun, moon, and stars would bow to him, and his father Jacob, angrily recognizing the implication of such a dream, said, "Shall I and thy mother and thy brethren indeed come to bow down ourselves to thee to the earth?" (Genesis 37:10).

One day when Joseph went to his brothers where they were feeding the flock, they took Joseph and stripped him of his coat, cast him into a pit, and sold him to a traveling company of Midianites, who took him down to Egypt. There he became a servant in Potiphar's house. Following domestic problems in the home which set Joseph in a bad light to the master of the house, Joseph was thrown into prison for a period of two years.

But God was with him and brought him before Pharaoh to interpret his dreams, and from this incident Joseph was made food administrator over all the land of Egypt. Seven years of great plenty were followed by years of dire famine. Nations round about Egypt suffered, and people would come into Egypt to buy grain from the granaries in which Joseph had stored food during the good years. Among the hungry who came were Joseph's brethren. They thought Joseph had died long before, and perhaps because of his dress, his language, and his demeanor, they did not recognize him when first they met.

The day came when the brothers traveled again into Egypt to buy food, and Joseph invited them to his home. After sending all the servants out of the room, Joseph stood before his brethren to reveal himself:

> And he said, I am Joseph your brother, whom ye sold into Egypt. Now therefore be not grieved, nor angry with yourselves, that ye sold me hither: for God did send me before you to preserve life (Genesis 45:4, 5).

With great emotion Joseph clasped each brother to himself and wept on his neck and kissed him. They in turn expressed the sorrow in their hearts for the maltreatment given to Joseph years before, and were amazed at the forgiving spirit he showed them.

Just as Joseph received ill treatment at the hands of his brethren, and later had a glorious reconciliation, so Jesus Christ received hatred and scorn from His brethren, and is looking forward to a reconciliation.

> Behold, he cometh with clouds; and every eye shall see him, and they also which pierced him (Revelation 1:7).

> And I will pour upon the house of David, and upon the inhabitants of Jerusalem, the spirit of grace and of supplication: and they shall look upon me whom they have pierced, and they shall mourn for him, as one mourneth for his only son, and shall be in bitterness for him, as one that is in bitterness for his firstborn (Zechariah 12:10).

The import of many Scriptures is that Christ comes at the crucial moment to deliver Israel from surrounding armies that threaten to annihilate her; and when the people see that their deliverer is the

One whom they put to death long ago, their sorrow and mourning will know no bounds. Zechariah 13: 8, 9 indicates that in the holocaust of the Tribulation period two-thirds of the people of Palestine will be destroyed, but the third part will be spared by the Lord, and this remnant will turn to the Lord in a day and receive Him as their Messiah.

The prophet Daniel shows it will take only a few weeks for the Lord to bring order out of chaos, to set up His reign upon earth, to delegate proper authority in every area, and to start Israel on its long-awaited era of peace and prosperity.

When Jesus reigns from Jerusalem, His law shall go forth in all the nations of the world. Israel shall become the head of the nations instead of the tail. The government by the Lord shall not only be over that little land, but "of the increase of his government and peace there shall be no end, upon the throne of David, and upon his kingdom, to order it, and to establish it with judgment and with justice from henceforth even for ever" (Isaiah 9:7).

7 Coming to Rule the Gentiles

We have shown that Jesus Christ is coming to catch the Church into the air to be with himself as His own special companion. Then His ministry in judgment was set forth in the plagues, vials of wrath, and trumpet judgments of the Tribulation. This was followed by His coming as the promised Messiah, the King of the Jews.

However, God has a grander program in mind than to place His Son over only one nation in the land of Palestine. He has in mind that His Son shall rule this entire planet in righteousness, and bring about an era of peace and plenty that will last 1,000 years until God is ready to usher in still another program in His universe.

The Scriptures that indicate such a kingdom on earth are too voluminous to be presented in their entirety. No doubt Israel was first in mind when God said, "I have set my king upon my holy hill of Zion" (Psalm 2:6). But there can be no mistaking the meaning of the prophecy of Isaiah,

Arise, shine; for thy light is come, and the glory of the Lord is risen upon thee. For, behold, the darkness shall cover the earth, and gross darkness the people: but the Lord shall arise upon thee, and his glory shall be seen upon thee. And the Gentiles shall come to thy light, and kings to the brightness of thy rising (60:1-3).

Just before our Lord's return to this earth a usurper whom we think of as Antichrist will assume the dominion of earthly power. He will be the choice of the unregenerate of the earth. His dominion will be greater than that of any other monarch in history. He shall think to change times and laws, and shall have power over the treasures of gold and silver. Military arms shall stand behind him in his quest for world rulership. But the Antichrist is not God's choice to rule and reign over this world. God is against all unrighteousness, and in the rule of the Antichrist evil shall reach its overflow. God is against sin in any man, and in the Tribulation the cup of iniquity spills over.

Sin is not going to have the last word in this world, for God is determined that the world is not going to be lost to Him forever. Christ died to redeem it, and the day will come when He shall see the fruits of victory in a world restored to Edenic beauty and peace.

Behold, a King shall reign in righteousness, and princes shall rule in judgment. And a man shall be as a hiding place from the wind, and a covert from the tempest; as rivers of water in a dry place, as the shadow of a great rock in a weary land (Isaiah 32:1, 2).

A Greater than Solomon

When Solomon, the son of David, came to the throne, God asked him, "What shall I give thee?" And Solomon replied, "Lord, I want wisdom to rule this, thy people." Because he asked for wisdom instead of riches and personal honor, God gave him his heart's desire, and added to him more glory and riches than those possessed by any earthly monarch before or since.

His wisdom became renowned in the courts of all other kingdoms, until kings and queens and rulers of all rank came to hear his wisdom and be taught at his feet. The queen of Sheba heard of his fame and came to speak with him. She witnessed the grandeur of his court, the happiness of his servants, and the peace that pervaded his realm. She heard wisdom and understanding from him that astounded her, and acknowledged before she left for her homeland that his wisdom had been much talked about, though "the half was not told me."

When Jesus spoke of judgment to come, He mentioned the coming of Sheba's queen to hear the wisdom of Solomon, and added, "A greater than Solomon is here" (Matthew 12:42). While Solomon's wisdom was a sanctified common sense, it was said of our Lord, "In [Him] are hid all the treasures of wisdom and knowledge" (Colossians 2:3). For every sinner who ever came to God for help, wisdom was offered to lift and strengthen him. For every Christian who has had a time of testing and trouble, infinite wisdom has been found in the presence of Christ to take him through the test. While Solomon is considered the wisest among men, his wisdom was as nothing compared to that of the Son of God.

It has been estimated by those who practice jurisprudence that there are 35 million laws in the world. Men are forever framing new laws to solve problems, and most of them take the form of restraints to curb man's sinful tendencies. Jesus Christ gave two laws which, if lived up to by all men, would make living conditions like heaven upon earth. They are: (1) "Thou shalt love the Lord thy God with all thy heart, and with all thy soul, and with all thy mind, and with all thy strength" (Mark 12:30). (2) "Thou shalt love thy neighbor as thyself" (Matthew 19:19). All righteousness which God expects from human hearts, as brought forth in the writings of the Lawgiver and the Prophets, is comprehended in those two laws.

While a greater than Solomon is here in wisdom, it must also be said that a greater than Solomon is here in vengeance. When Solomon took the throne upon the death of his father, David, there was some housecleaning to be done in his nation. Rebels had to be dealt with quickly so that others might fear and tremble at the consequences of rebellion. In 1 Kings 2 we read that a man named Shimei would not obey the commands of King Solomon, so the king commanded Benaiah, the captain of the host, to fall upon him with the sword and kill him.

Again, Joab was a captain under David, but after David's death he followed the usurper, Adonijah. So Benaiah, the executioner, was commanded to fall upon him and kill him with the sword also.

The news soon spread throughout the land that the king meant business. He would tolerate no form of evil that would mar the peace and prosperity of his kingdom.

Several significant statements are brought forth in the Word of God to show that rebellion will not be tolerated under the coming reign of Christ. If Solomon seemed to have a heavy hand upon his enemies, think carefully of the heavy hand of Christ upon any tyranny that rears itself under His rule. The second psalm of David states, concerning His reign:

> Thou shalt break them with a rod of iron; thou shalt dash them in pieces like a potter's vessel (v. 9).

Those who would have any thoughts of rebellion are instructed to

> Kiss the Son, lest he be angry, and ye perish from the way, when his wrath is kindled but a little (v. 12).

The prophet Zechariah confirms the enforced reign of Christ during the coming millennial era. He stated that all nations left after the holocaust of Armageddon shall go up to Jerusalem from year to year to worship the King, the Lord of hosts, and to keep the Feast of Tabernacles. No doubt representatives of all countries, ambassadors, and rulers from all parts of the globe shall come to Jerusalem to pay homage to King Jesus, to bring Him gifts, and to hear the law from His mouth. However, Zechariah adds that if a nation refuses to send representatives to Jerusalem to see the Lord, "even upon them shall be no rain." He illustrates what is meant in 14:18, 19:

> And if the family of Egypt go not up, and come not, they have no rain; there shall be the plague, wherewith the Lord will smite the heathen that come not up to keep the feast of tabernacles. This shall be the punishment of Egypt, and the punishment of all nations that come not up to keep the feast of tabernacles.

Everyone who looks forward to peace on earth can shout Hallelujah over such prophecies, for it simply means that righteousness shall not be stepped on forever. It shall come to the fore, and the centuries of sinning shall come to an end.

> I will punish the world for their evil, and the wicked for their iniquity; and I will cause the arrogancy of the proud to cease, and will lay low the haughtiness of the terrible. (Isaiah 13:11).

A greater than Solomon shall reign not only in

wisdom and vengeance, but also in peace. What an elusive thing is peace. Nations have sought for it diligently. Men have given their lives in its pursuit. In recent years the tendency has been to arm for war while suing for peace, and in all their searching there has been the element of distrust.

No nation ever had such quietness and rest within its borders as Israel under Solomon. He had peace on all sides round about him. "Judah and Israel dwelt safely, every man under his vine and under his fig tree, from Dan even to Beer-sheba, all the days of Solomon" (1 Kings 4:25). Happiness reigned. The wisdom of the king and his counselors sought the welfare of all in the realm, and brought each family a degree of affluence that made for contentment.

But, again, a greater than Solomon is here. The coming of Jesus Christ to earth will mean peace and prosperity not only for Israel but for the entire earth.

Even when on earth the first time, Jesus was bringing peace to those who followed Him. "My peace give I unto you: not as the world giveth, give I unto you" (John 14:27) was his legacy to those who followed Him.

His first utterance in the Upper Room after His resurrection was "Peace be unto you." And every Christian, walking as a pilgrim and a stranger in this present evil world, is to have the peace that passes all understanding in his heart as he walks with God. Peace is one of the glorious character traits that Jesus wishes for all people. In His coming reign of righteousness, peace shall spread throughout the earth.

The Scriptures on this subject are almost innumerable. They portray a world free from war under Christ's reign. The billions of dollars now spent on modern armaments shall then be diverted to education, the removal of poverty, the building of architectural wonders, and the spreading of the Good News about Christ. Manufacturers of armaments will turn their talents from weapons of war to implements of argiculture.

> They shall beat swords into plowshares, and their spears into pruning hooks (Isaiah 2:4).

Places like West Point and Annapolis where the art of war is learned will be phased out, for "nation shall not lift up sword against nation, neither shall they learn war any more" (Isaiah 2:4).

For centuries men have sought various kinds of relief for the maladies of the body. Our drugstores offer remedies for every conceivable type of physical problem; and the strides made in surgical practices have been nothing short of phenomenal, even to the transplanting of vital organs of the body. Laboratories are working night and day to find further remedies that will add to man's longevity and make him more comfortable in this world.

But here again it will be said a greater than Solomon is here. For in the days when Christ rules this world,

> . . . the eyes of the blind shall be opened, and the ears of the deaf shall be unstopped. Then shall the lame man leap as a hart, and the tongue of the dumb sing: for in the wilderness shall waters break out, and streams in the desert (Isaiah 35:5, 6).

Yes, streams of healing and blessing shall flow as the knowledge of the Lord is spread throughout the earth. People will not have to be asked if they know the Lord. All shall know Him from the least to the greatest, for the knowledge of Him, and of His glorious righteousness, shall cover the earth as the waters cover the sea.

No country has ever been more beautiful, or more prosperous, or more peaceful than Israel under the reign of Solomon; and if one can imagine these elements for all countries on earth, then we may grasp in part the glories to come for this earth.

Rulership: the Church's Inheritance

Where the Bible says "we shall be kings and priests unto God" (Revelation 1:6) the implication is that the Church will be in a position of rulership, and also have the task of leading in worship, for that is an important part of priesthood. Just as a young heir to some important title is specially trained for his future responsibilities, so the Holy Spirit is teaching and training us for the day when we shall enter upon our inheritance, and the glory in us shall be revealed in the coming age.

What then is the glory? Arthur Wallis said, "It is the revealing of the sons of God. Paul paints the picture of the creation groaning with a desire, breathless with expectation, for this moment for which all the past ages were but a preparation, when God will display to the wondering eyes of the whole universe His masterpiece."

The poetry and hymns of the centuries have endeavored to describe the glory of the time when Christ returns and ushers in His righteous reign. When that day dawns and that hour strikes—when the heir of the universe steps onto the throne—He will not be alone, for His fellow heirs will be with Him. He is coming to be "glorified in his saints . . . in all them that believe" (2 Thessalonians 1:10).

The entire creation was brought into bondage through man's sin, and only the final redemption of man will effect its release into glorious liberty. This age is only a probationary period for the believer, in preparation for the true age of service to come. In the Parable of the Ten Pounds, the master, on his return, told the first servant, whose one pound had gained ten pounds, "You have been faithful . . . in a very little, you shall have authority over ten cities" (Luke 19:17, *Amplified*). From being steward over a modest sum (a few pounds, which his master describes as a very little) he finds himself ruler of a sizable province of his master's kingdom. The principle on which the Lord will determine His appointments in that day is now operating. He who is faithful in a very little is faithful also in much. The day of reckoning and the day of rewards will come soon.

Let us remember, then, that the world to come has not been promised to the angels, nor to future generations who shall be born upon the earth. It has been promised to Christian people who are faithful and loyal to their present tasks. We are now qualifying for our positions in the Kingdom. The crowns we wear will be earned, and not received simply as souvenirs. No one will receive authority who has not been made ready for it. Our final preparation for rulership will be the receiving of our glorified bodies, and the judgment of our works; for the works of all believers shall be judged, that each may receive according to that which he has done.

It is hard to imagine a world where righteousness covers the earth. We have been reared in a world soaked in liquor, where profanity is common, where gambling is legal, where tensions and frictions are the lot of all. We live in a world where half of its inhabitants go to bed hungry every night, and have little or no clothing. Our world is plagued by earthquakes, hurricanes, tornadoes, floods, and other ravages of nature. We have never known a time when some serious problem was not upsetting our dreams and plans.

But think of a world of honesty and integrity, where all nations know the Lord, where love is the dominant motive in the affairs of men. Then David's ideal shall be realized on earth, as he mentioned in Psalm 144:12-15:

> That our sons may be as plants grown up in their youth; that our daughters may be as corner stones, polished after the similitude of a palace:
>
> That our garners may be full, affording all manner of store; that our sheep may bring forth thousands and ten thousands in our streets:
>
> That our oxen may be strong to labor; that there be no breaking in, nor going out; that there be no complaining in our streets.
>
> Happy is that people, that is in such a case: yea, happy is that people, whose God is the Lord.

The Golden Age

Many are the prophecies of a coming age of peace and prosperity. During the Millennium there will be no men in military uniform, no military camps operating, not a cent spent for armaments. All nations shall be at peace with one another, and all the resources of earth be available for men's enjoyment and for the manufacture of useful articles. It will be an age of no poverty, no wastelands, no droughts, no crop failures, no floods. Even the wild animals will be tame and harmless. Where do we find such information? In the Word of God! One could spend hours reading the prophecies foretelling and describing this future golden age of redemption.

Marvelous changes shall take place in the human kingdom, the animal kingdom, and the vegetable kingdom. All three shall be greatly affected by the reign of Christ, for all three came under the curse when sin entered the world.

One of the chief characteristics of the millennial reign will be peace, the dream of the nations. It has eluded men because of the lusts and passions of their hearts, and it can be shown that wars have increased rather than decreased with the advance of civilization.

Over 8,000 treaties of peace were drawn up between 1500 B.C. and A.D. 1860, and the average period that each remained in force was only two years. In spite of all those treaties, according to the Society of International Law in London there have been only 268 years of world peace in the past 4,000 years.

In 1928, 15 nations ratified the Pact of Paris, and by 1934, 63 governments had signed and ratified it. Many thought the end of war was in sight. But our world has not had one full year without a war since the Pact came into being. Men without Christ will never know peace. "There is no peace, saith my God, to the wicked" (Isaiah 57:21). "The way of peace they know not" (Isaiah 59:8).

The Bible predicts a coming time of peace and prosperity lasting 1,000 years. Many there are who say that Christ will never rule on this earth, and that there will never be a Millennium, but God speaks so much about it that a larger body of prophecies is devoted to the Millennium than to any other single subject.

This period will commence immediately after the return of Jesus Christ on earth. He will defeat Antichrist and his armies at Armageddon. The beast and the false prophet will be cast alive into the lake of fire, and their followers will be slain (Revelation 19:20, 21). Satan will be imprisoned in the bottomless pit for 1,000 years. These activities of Christ will remove the spiritual forces that have promoted sin in the world and lay the groundwork for peace during His reign.

Jesus spoke of His coming in glory and His reign: "When the Son of man shall come in his glory, and all the holy angels with him, then shall he sit upon the throne of his glory" (Matthew 25:31).

Christ's return was described by Zechariah (14:3, 9):

> Then shall the Lord go forth, and fight against those nations, as when he fought in the day of battle. . . . And the Lord shall be King over all the earth: in that day shall there be one Lord, and his name one.

Material prosperity will characterize the Millennium. Farmers today will tell you that farming is a gamble. Inclement weather, during sowing or during harvest, is always a hazard. They contend with snow, frost, hail, wind, upsets in the market, variations in the law of supply and demand. However, the material prosperity promised for the coming era is almost beyond belief.

> For the seed shall be prosperous; the vine shall give her fruit, and the ground shall give her increase, and the heavens shall give their dew; and I will cause the remnant of this people to possess all these things (Zechariah 8:12).

> Fear not, O land; be glad and rejoice: for the Lord will do great things. Be not afraid, ye beasts of the field: for the pastures of the wilderness do spring, for the tree beareth her fruit, the fig tree and the vine do yield their strength. . . . And the floors shall be full of wheat, and the vats shall overflow of wine and oil. And ye shall eat in plenty, and be satisfied, and praise the name of the Lord your God, that hath dealt wondrously with you (Joel 2:21, 22, 24, 26).

> I will call for the corn, and will increase it, and lay no famine upon you. And I will multiply the fruit of the tree, and the increase of the field, that ye shall receive no more reproach of famine among the heathen. . . . And the desolate land shall be tilled, whereas it lay desolate in the sight of all that passed by. And they shall say, This land that was desolate is become like the garden of Eden (Ezekiel 36:29, 30, 34, 35).

Summing up many of the verses that deal with this prosperity, we find that rainfall will be abundant; trees will bear fruit; fertility of the earth shall increase;

there shall be no malnutrition or death from famine; granaries will be full of wheat; wine and oil will fill the vats to overflowing; the planted seed will produce. The cycles of sowing and reaping will no longer be a gamble, but will have an assured regularity.

Righteousness and true holiness shall characterize the Millennium. Many millions of sinners will have been killed during the horrors of the Tribulation, and those who enter the Millennium will enter in the fear of the Lord.

It has been the experience of our own lifetime and of history that the moral tendencies of a nation are often patterned after its leadership. Under the evil reigns of Manasseh and Amon, Israel went to the depths of idolatry; but under the godly Josiah a great move toward the worship of God was seen. Corruption in political leaders in America in recent years has spawned a permissiveness toward crime, evil literature, the liquor industry, and other related evils, all of which tends downward and away from the morality taught in the Scriptures.

It will be different under the reign of Christ. His ruling with a rod of iron will mean enforced obedience to His righteous laws. Flagrant sin during His reign will not be tolerated. He will deal with violators quickly and with finality, with no appeal, and will show no respect of persons.

The Kingdom of the Stone

In Daniel 2 we read that the awesome image God revealed to Nebuchadnezzar was destroyed by the coming of an irresistible stone that smote the image on its feet and ground the entire structure to powder. In turn the stone grew to be a great mountain that filled the entire earth. What magnificent imagery!

Let us look briefly at this dream of the Babylonian king. He saw a monstrous image with a head of gold, with shoulders and breast of silver, with belly and thighs of brass, with legs of iron, and with feet of iron mixed with clay. While viewing the image he noted a stone that was cut out of the mountain without hands; it came with great speed and smote the image, destroying it completely.

The prophet Daniel told the king in some detail that the image represented a succession of world empires . . . Babylon, Medo-Persia, Greece, and Rome, and that in the latter days of the fourth kingdom the God of heaven would set up a kingdom that would supplant these other kingdoms—a kingdom that would last forever.

We are most interested in the "stone cut out of the mountain without hands." Who or what is this stone? We are not in darkness concerning it, for the imagery of the Scriptures indicates the stone to be none other than the Lord Jesus Christ.

In Genesis 49:24 we read:

> But his bow abode in strength, and the arms of his hands were made strong by the hands of the mighty God of Jacob: (from thence is the shepherd, the stone of Israel).

Again in Isaiah 28:16 we read,

> Therefore thus saith the Lord God, Behold I lay in Zion for a foundation a stone, a tried stone, a precious corner stone, a sure foundation . . .

This passage was used again in Romans 9:33 and 1 Peter 2:6. The Stone is Christ, and upon this rock, upon the deity of the Son of God, the Church is built.

Again in 1 Corinthians 10:4 Paul stated,

> . . . they drank of that spiritual Rock that followed them: and that Rock was Christ.

The prophet told the king the approximate time in history when the kingdom of the Stone would be set up. The event would happen when all empires have ceased, in the days of the ten toes of the image, in the days of a many-nationed world. There will never be another world empire before Christ comes. Napoleon tried to establish one and left half his troops in the snows of Russia, and thousands more at Waterloo. England tried to found one, but the colonial empire became a commonwealth—a cooperative group of self-governing countries with close ties to the crown. In recent years superpowers have competed for world leadership, but none has held the civilized world in its grasp such as the four empires mentioned in Daniel's Book. Today we have a multinationed world of law and administration mixed with the passing whims and fancies of the people. According to the revelation of God, the Stone shall strike the feet of the image when the world sweep of empire has passed away and when the sovereign, separate nations of the world are divided as they are today into East, West, American, European, Asiatic, African . . . in those days the Stone shall strike, and we live in the momentous time when the God of heaven is about to set up a Kingdom that shall never pass away.

At first the Stone will destroy, The composition of earthly powers as they have been must be shattered and broken and ground to pieces. Religious and civil rulers will fail. Monarchies, dictatorships, parliamentary forms of governments, democracies, all shall be ground to powder before the coming of the government of the Stone; for in all of them is the flagrant display of the evil in human hearts that disqualifies mankind from ruling God's earth, but in the kingdom of the Stone there will be justice in righteousness and true equity.

Absolute dictatorships such as that which Nebuchadnezzar exercised over Babylon will be no more. Military governments, like that of Alexander in Greece, will no longer exist. The Roman form of government with laws and rules of jurisprudence will cease, for such is too often born out of the whims of powerful men, and, lacking true righteousness, is subject to change with the passing of time. The coming of the Stone shall end the conglomeration of governments in human history. Like "the chaff of the summer threshing floor" they shall pass away, and the world of politics and power as we have known it shall be no more.

Following the destroying ministry of the Stone will come a restoration such as the world has never known. The God of heaven is planning a kingdom for this earth that will set forth His benevolence toward all nations, but the old must be destroyed before the new can appear. The entire planet must be purged and renovated, for "the Stone became a great mountain that filled the whole earth." This imagery of the Stone's becoming a great mountain and filling the whole earth is a picture of Christ's literal reign on this earth during the Millennium. "And in the days of these kings [ten toes of the image] shall the God of heaven set up a kingdom, which shall never be destroyed: and the kingdom shall not be left to other people, but it shall break in pieces and consume all these kingdoms, and it shall stand for ever" (Daniel 2:44).

Here, then, is a unique and powerful kingdom to come. The God of heaven sets it up. No human agency is in evidence, for the Stone "is cut out without hands" and is brought forth by some invisible, superhuman power. Christ is the Stone. His being "cut out without hands" indicates His coming by the power of the Holy Spirit through the Virgin Birth apart from man's efforts. The "mountain" from which He is cut is none other than the eternal permanency of the immortal Godhead, for mountains always tell of deity and omnipotence. It entirely ends and supersedes all human dominions, sweeps them away, and takes their place.

This kingdom is eternal and fills the whole earth, something that has never been true of other kingdoms though they were spoken of as being universal. Human dominion passes from one ruler to another, but the kingdom of the Stone "shall not be left to other people," for it shall be eternally in the grasp of the Lord Jesus Christ.

Our Lord speaks of himself as "The stone which the builders rejected," a reference to Psalm 118:22, 23. "The stone which the builders refused is become the head stone of the corner. This is the Lord's doing; it is marvelous in our eyes." During the building of Solomon's temple the parts of the building were prepared, measured, fitted, and brought to the site of construction. One stone was in a prominent place at the building site and always seemed to be in the way. Workmen finally pushed it out of the way and it was shoved down over an embankment where, during the many months of construction, it was grown over with weeds. When the time came to lay the cornerstone the proper stone was not to be seen, and it was found that the one rolled away by the workers was the one that perfectly fitted the corner. Thus, "The stone which the builders refused is become the head stone of the corner."

How sad that throughout the governments on earth

Christ has been forgotten. He is not asked to be at the councils, or at treaty signings, or at similar government functions. His name may be invoked, but merely out of courtesy, and sometimes a hymn is sung to give a religious touch to a secular event. But His wisdom and knowledge are not sought after by the world in general. He is the head of the corner, and has been shoved out of the way; consequently the structure man builds for himself is never completed.

To the nation of Israel, Christ has been "a stone of stumbling, and a rock of offense" (1 Peter 2:8). They fell upon "this Stone" and were broken. They stumbled at His word. They rejected Him when He declared himself to be God's Son, and the New Testament and the unfolding of history have shown them to be a people "scattered and peeled," a proverb and byword among the nations.

To the Church, or the company of believers in His name, His relation is of another character. He is still "the Stone," but His people come to Him, "as unto a living stone, disallowed indeed of men, but chosen of God, and precious" (1 Peter 2:4).

While a Stone of stumbling to some, and a living Stone to others, He is also a Stone that falls upon those rebellious powers who stand opposed to Him when He comes the second time, and grinds them to powder. His first coming was that of a meek Lamb, a gentle Saviour, weeping over the hardness of men's hearts. No matter their hostility to Him; He bore it patiently and did not insult or persecute in turn. But everywhere in the Scriptures He has made known the fact that the time is coming when the measure of suffering and forbearance will be filled up; when this Stone shall take on the activities of judgment; when "the Lord shall go forth as a mighty man, he shall stir up jealously like a man of war: he shall cry, yea, roar; he shall prevail against his enemies" (Isaiah 42:13).

Daniel closed his interpretation concerning the succession of world empires followed by the kingdom of the Stone by saying, "The dream is certain, and the interpretation thereof sure" (Daniel 2:45). Nothing can alter the decrees of heaven; they are eternal. From the beginning of man's reign on earth, God has made it known that a kingdom is coming that shall break in pieces and consume all other kingdoms, and that shall stand forever—a kingdom of which the God-man shall be the Head and King. All dispensations have looked forward to the coming of such a kingdom, and all ages have waited for this grand and glorious culmination.

8 Signs of His Coming

Signs and portents seemed very important to the people of Jesus' day, especially such signs as would indicate some great divine intervention in the affairs of men. Paul stated that in contrast with those who received the gospel by faith, the Jews "require a sign."

Also when Jesus had given His audience the startling news that every stone of the temple would be thrown down, they immediately asked, "What shall be the sign of thy coming, and of the end of the age?"

It may be stated that no signs are to be looked for to indicate the nearness of the Rapture of the Church. But the signs preceding the coming of Jesus to this earth again are many. Such was one of the major themes of the Old Testament prophets, and such was the burden of the Olivet discourse (Matthew 24). A person who is knowledgeable concerning world affairs or even the casual reader of the Bible would have to be willfully blind to miss the many activities of our modern world that indicate that a divine intervention is about to take place.

If we were to choose two or three outstanding signs of the coming of Christ, we would have to place the rise of Russia among those signs. In 1917 there was a revolution, and at the end of World War I Russia was a broken nation, her major cities in ruins, and much of her manpower lost in the war. At that time no one dreamed that within 40 years the nation would rank as a superpower, with nearly half the globe under its actual military heel.

Chapters 38 and 39 of the Book of the prophet Ezekiel speak specifically of Russia in the latter days. In the time when Israel is said to be dwelling safely in the land of Palestine, Russia is to invade the land "to take a spoil, and to take a prey." There was no possible way in which this prophecy could be fulfilled before this present generation, because Israel was not a nation in Palestine, but was still scattered throughout the earth. However, in 1948 Israel was declared a nation, the Israeli flag was raised, and nations of the world began to recognize the infant nation as a political entity. Today for the first time in world history Russia could fulfill the predictions of the prophet.

"To take a spoil and to take a prey" are the reasons the prophet gave for the coming invasion. Through remarkable Jewish ingenuity the land of Palestine is becoming a magnificent land. Thousands of acres of oranges, grapefruit, olives, and various grains supply the needs of the people and leave a surplus for export. Trainloads of produce are hauled to seaports for shipment to many parts of the world. Oil has been discovered. Minerals from the Dead Sea have given rise to multimillion-dollar exports, and the potash deposits in that area alone could furnish the world with enough fertilizer for the next 200 years. Magnificent homes and public buildings are increasing in number. The land is becoming like the garden of Eden in many places, and tourism has become a major business. Yes, Israel is "a spoil and a prey" to be desired. In his book *Prophecy Made Plain for Times Like These*, Carl G. Johnson quotes Dr. John F. Walvoord of the Dallas Theological Seminary:

> An invasion of Israel in the 20th century by Russia seems a likely development in the end of the age. The fact that Russia has risen to such power in our day sets up a situation which, coupled with Israel's return to the land, establishes the basic conditions set forth by Ezekiel for the fulfillment of his prophecy. The situation of Israel dwelling in unwalled villages is a modern situation, not true in the ancient past. The stage is being set for the final drama of the end of the age.

By April 1973 it was reported in the *U. S. News and World Report* that the USSR had 1,590 intercontinental ballistic missiles, 10,000 surface-to-air missiles, 48 nuclear missile submarines, 3,000 interceptor aircraft, and 64 antiballistic missile systems. Because of this awesome array of power, former world powers like Britain, France, and Germany have frantically sought alliances to protect their interests. The United States has been engaged in a series of meetings for a Strategic Arms Limitation Treaty with Russia; and expressions such as peaceful coexistence, détente, and nuclear balance have become common because of the search for a means to avert a possible holocaust.

We see, in all these things, the rise of Russia in the 20th century as a direct fulfillment of many prophetic Scriptures. The stage is being set for the literal fulfillment of Ezekiel's prophecies in the 38th and 39th chapters of his Book.

Departure from the Faith

Paul stated, "In the last days some shall depart from

the faith." You cannot depart from something you do not possess; therefore the prophecy refers to many who started to serve the Lord but fell by the wayside. Every generation has had or seen a denial of God outside the established church, but our generation is witnessing a denial of God within the established church. Such terms as Christian atheists, higher criticism, the death of God have arisen to cast doubts upon the veracity of the Scriptures.

Modernism in a greater or lesser degree seems to permeate every major denomination. Numerous religious leaders have voiced their denial of the deity of Christ, the substitutionary atonement, the verbal inspiration of the Bible, the Virgin Birth, the physical resurrection of the body, and especially the second coming of Christ. Departure from the faith, or backsliding as it is commonly called, has always been a characteristic of all periods of church history, for the Church has never seen 100 percent of its converts walking in true holiness and faithful service; but the movement away from the foundations of the faith has mushroomed in our times. Today it constitutes a fulfillment of the prophetic Word, and a sure sign that the return of Jesus to this earth will be soon.

The Ecumenical Movement

The word *ecumenical* suggests one large religious body with its influence embracing the inhabited earth. Church leaders began to converse about the possibilities of a religious amalgamation in 1910 at the world conference on missionary cooperation in Edinburgh. The subject was on the agenda at the 1925 Christian council in Stockholm, Sweden. Again it was made a part of the business in 1927 at the world conference on faith and order in Lausanne, Switzerland.

Definite action to bring about a World Council of Churches took place in Amsterdam on August 23, 1948, significantly the year that Israel became a nation. The chairman at that meeting said, "The primary object of the World Council is the effective welding of the Christian churches of the world into a single unit."

Some believe the ecumenical movement is symbolized in Revelation 17 as a harlot riding a scarlet-colored beast; for this forerunner of a world church professes faithfulness to Christ, but in reality is unfaithful to Him. Thus she is in contrast to the Bride of Christ who is "without spot or wrinkle" and whose members "made their garments white in the blood of the Lamb."

In my opinion this superchurch will be destroyed by the Antichrist midway through the Tribulation (Revelation 17:16, 17). She will prove to be worthless as a moral force, for her concentration is on economics, politics, and sociology rather than on holy living and the exaltation of Christ. Her uselessness will be apparent, and the political powers of the Tribulation period shall make war upon this superchurch and destroy her.

Such destruction is spelled out in the Scriptures. They will "make her desolate" by withdrawing political and military support. They "will make her naked" by taking away all her outward glamor and attractiveness. "They will eat her flesh" by seizing all her wealth and leaving her standing like a religious skeleton. And "they will burn her with fire," meaning that her buildings, shrines, altars, images, and finery will be destroyed or confiscated. The cry John hears in Revelation 18:4 is "Come out of her my people, that ye be not partakers of her sins, and that ye receive not of her plagues." Every true Christian should separate himself from this unscriptural and apostate system. The present trend of criticism and liberal teaching in so many churches seems to be preparing the way for the final apostate religious system. The widespread character of the present apostasy in the visible church, the union of various groups into larger denominations without regard to doctrinal consideration, the increasing openness of Catholic and Protestant groups toward each other, the constant intrusion of church bodies into political affairs, and the replacing of the authority of the Bible with the presumed authority of man all seem to say very loudly that the coming of a climax is not far off, and the coming of the Lord is near.

Four World Power Blocs

With man's ability to wage war in an ever more terrifying manner has also come the desire to be surrounded with allies; and this has led to the formation of massive power blocs such as the North Atlantic Treaty Organization, the South-East Asia Treaty Organization, and similar military alliances. This again is a fulfillment in these last days of great prophecies of the Bible.

The prophet Daniel, when speaking of the wars that followed the breakup of the Grecian Empire into four parts, continually refers to the king of the south and the king of the north. And when his prophecy leaps from those wars to the time of the end, he continues to use the same terms (Daniel 11:40).

In brief, the power blocs of the end-time may be summarized as follows:

To the north of Israel these last days have seen the rise of Russia and her allies, which Ezekiel 38 tells us will include Persia, Ethiopia, Libya, Gomer, and

Togarmah, which many scholars believe is Turkey. Other nations in this bloc are included in the phrase "and all his bands: and many people with thee" (Ezekiel 38:5).

To the south of Israel the land of Egypt has come out of obscurity to be a military force to be reckoned with in the last days. The formation of the United Arab Republic includes several oil-rich nations that have consistently looked to Egypt for leadership. Together they have openly avowed their determination to push Israel into the sea.

In the Far East another power bloc is arising, known in Revelation 16 as the "armies of the east." In recent years both China and India have joined the nuclear club, and China has boasted of her ability to field an army of 200 million men by herself. Furthermore, superhighways are being planned that will make it possible for massive armies to move toward the Middle East. The use of the plural word "armies" when speaking of this Eastern power would indicate a uniting of forces prior to Armageddon.

To the west of Israel we have seen the growth of the European Common Market, a combine of nations that have given their hand to each other for industrial and trade reasons, and whose long-range plans envisage political union and a common currency. This Common Market is still in its formative stage. It is significant that the countries involved were once a part of the Old Roman Empire, and that Daniel prophesied that "in the latter days" the Roman Empire would be revived so that out of it "ten kings shall arise." These 10 kings, or union of 10 countries, probably would become the power base for the coming Antichrist.

Let us look at the rise of the Common Market, which

foreshadows Antichrist's Empire, and the rising of which indicates the near return of the Lord Jesus.

America's former Secretary of State, Dean Acheson, said, "The success of the movement toward unity in the West of Europe is no longer in doubt. A common currency and political unity are on the way."

In 1958 six countries—Belgium, France, Holland, Italy, Luxembourg, and West Germany—established the European Economic Community, commonly known as the Common Market. On January 22, 1972, it was announced that Britain, Ireland, Norway and Denmark would enter the merger, but Norway withdrew, leaving nine nations as members. In Britain public opinion is greatly divided with respect to the advisability of the merger.

The merger of nations within this economic community can rival the USSR and the United States in trade, representing a working group of nations numbering 255 million people.

Jean Monnet, one of the chief architects of the Common Market, stated that the group would be limited to 10 nations, and this is most significant in the light of prophecy, for Daniel speaks of 10 horns that grew out of the beast (the Roman Empire in the last days), and 10 toes on the feet of the image as seen by King Nebuchadnezzar (which represented the succession of world empires). The prophet Daniel stated also that from among the 10 horns that shall arise will also come a "little horn," a man who will become a powerful ruler. He will be characterized by his terrible blasphemy against God, and his persecution of the Jews.

If such a union is materializing, and if the powerful Antichrist is to arise as its head, then all these things happening in our political world indicate the soon return of the Lord Jesus Christ to this earth.

Paul-Henri Spaak, a former premier of Belgium, in a speech before the U.N. General Assembly, said:

> The truth is that the method of international committees has failed. What we need is a person, someone of the highest order of great experience, of great authority, of great energy; let him come, and let him come quickly . . . either a civilian or a military man, no matter what his nationality, who will cut all red tape, shove out of the way all committees, wake up all the people, and galvanize all governments into action. Let him come, and let him come quickly.

No doubt we are seeing the formative stages of that great western power that will appear after the return of Christ to earth; then the Rapture of the Church, so long looked for by the children of God, and which must take place before the endtime events, must be at hand.

Increase of Travel and Knowledge

Where Daniel said "many shall run to and fro, and knowledge shall be increased," the original wording gives the idea of a sudden knowledge explosion in the time of the end. No fewer than 15,000 scientific journals are being published regularly over the world, and it has been said that 90 percent of all scientists who ever lived are alive today, indicating the emphasis on research in laboratories and colleges. Not less than 90 percent of all drugs prescribed today were unknown 10 years ago. No less an authority than J. Robert Oppenheimer, who did so much research on nuclear fission, stated that half of all knowledge was acquired over 6,000 years, and the other half has been acquired in the last 15 years. At the present time there are approximately 20 million young people in the colleges of the world, and enough research is going on in laboratories each day to fill seven sets of the *Encyclopaedia Britannica*. A knowledge explosion has taken place.

Where the prophet says "many shall run to and fro" some translations of the Bible indicate that in the last days many shall run to and fro throughout the Book of Daniel, and knowledge of the Book of Daniel shall be increased. This is very true, for the unfolding of history has helped scholars learn more about the prophecies of Daniel than the prophet knew himself from his vantage point. The events of which Daniel prophesied had not taken place in his time, and we have the advantage of knowing how many of his predictions unfolded. His Book, which was sealed to him and to his generation, is more open to the believers of our time.

However, it is commonly accepted that the words "many shall run to and fro" refer to an explosion of travel in the last days, and such a trend in the last 50 years would confirm the accuracy of this prophecy. Horse-and-buggy days are still within the memory of many in this generation, and it has been a source of wonder and amazement how fast and how far the world has come in its mobility. A journey that took months at the turn of the 20th century is now but a matter of a few hours by jet plane. One of the early pioneers of the automobile stated that if a speed of 60 miles an hour were ever attained it would take people's breath away. Only a few years later people were driving on superhighways, in air-conditioned comfort, with a choice of radio music, at speeds approaching 100 miles an hour.

A World in Travail

After Jesus told of the coming of wars, rumors of

wars, famines, pestilences, earthquakes, and all manner of troubles that would increase before His second coming, He emphasized that these signs are the beginnings of sorrows. A. T. Robertson declared that the beginnings of sorrows means the beginning of travail; and the Greek word for sorrows, or travail, is *odin* and literally means birth pangs.

A new world is about to be born. Heaven's dawn is breaking, and the Daystar is rising. A new age that will last 1,000 years is about to be introduced. Just as human birth is accompanied by pain and travail, so the birth of a new world and new order is seeing the present distress and travail among the nations. Statesmen are running throughout the earth endeavoring to pour the oil of diplomacy on the troubled waters. The game of semantics goes on with pledges here and promises there. Toasts are drunk to each other's health and to an era of peace, but the travail goes on and the ferment and tension increase. When will they learn that the peace of the world is dependent upon the return of Jesus Christ to take the reins of government in His own hands? Christ is the forgotten man in world affairs, but His day will come, and His reign shall be glorious.

9 Israel: Key to the Endtime

At the first church council in Jerusalem (Acts 15) James presided and he stated that God was visiting the Gentiles to take out of them a people for His name. James indicated that, following this phase of God's program, the next phase would be to "build again the tabernacle of David, which is fallen down; and I will build again the ruins thereof, and I will set it up" (v. 16).

The "tabernacle of David" is a phrase indicating the nation of Israel as it was when the priesthood and ceremonial laws and temple worship were existing. Since A.D. 70, when Jerusalem was besieged, the temple torn down, and the ceremonies brought to an end, it may be said that the tabernacle of David "is fallen down."

The promises to Israel are for the rebuilding of the nation and the reestablishing of their temple. "After this I will return, and will build again the tabernacle . . . that the residue of men might seek after the Lord, and all the Gentiles, upon whom my name is called, saith the Lord . . ." (vv. 16, 17).

Before any major prophecy comes to pass God gives indications of its approaching fulfillment. Things are happening in our world showing forth the working of the divine hand in the affairs of men, and bringing to pass the will of God in spite of all that man can do.

It must be said that in spite of the declaration of Israel to be a nation in 1948, and the growth of the nation since that time, the tabernacle of David is still fallen; that is, most of the children of Israel are still scattered among the nations. But what we have seen since 1948 indicates that the rebuilding of the ruins of Israel is near, and in a small measure has begun. The ultimate fulfillment of the prophecy to rebuild national Israel will come when God is through taking out from among the nations a people for His name. For it is "after that" that Israel shall enjoy the promises and covenants that shall bring her to an exaltation among all nations.

Palestine and World War I

At the beginning of the 20th century there was not a single all-Jewish village in all of Palestine, and only about 25,000 Jews were scattered through the land. When World War I began in 1914 the Holy Land was held by the Turks. Out of Egypt marched a Brititish column toward the city of Jerusalem. These troops were led by General Edmund Henry Allenby, a Christian military man who, in his youth, had been taught to close his daily prayer with a plea for Israel: "Forget not Thine ancient people. Hasten the day when they shall be restored to Thy favor and to their land."

During the night, as he was preparing to take his troops into the city, he read his Bible and prayed earnestly; and God gave him a verse of Scripture, Isaiah 31:5: "As birds flying, so will the Lord of hosts defend Jerusalem; . . . and passing over he will preserve it." The next day, December 11, 1917, General Allenby sent wave after wave of planes low over the city. No bombs were dropped and not a shot was fired. The city easily fell to the British troops.

The Allenby Bridge, spanning the Jordan River, was built in commemoration of this victory, and at a reception in London the general remarked, "I never knew that God would give me the privilege of helping to answer my own childhood prayer."

During World War I another incident took place that aided greatly in opening Palestine to Jewish immigration. Britain could not get an adequate supply of wood alcohol for the production of acetone, needed to make explosives. The situation became critical until Dr. Chaim Weizmann, a Jewish professor, engaged in research into the production of synthetic acetone from starch, and undertook large-scale production of it. Because of this outstanding service to Britain, special honors were planned for him, but he declined them, stating that his only wish was for Palestine to be opened as a home for the Jew.

On November 2, 1917, Lord Balfour, the Foreign Secretary, wrote the following letter to Lord Rothschild, a wealthy British Jew:

Dear Lord Rothschild:

I have much pleasure in conveying to you, on behalf of His Majesty's Government, the following declaration of sympathy with Jewish Zionist aspirations, which has been submitted to, and approved by the cabinet.

His Majesty's Government view with favor the establishment in Palestine of a national home for the Jewish People, and will use their best endeavors to facilitate the achievement of this object, it being clearly understood that nothing shall be done which may prejudice the civil and religious rights of existing non-Jewish communities in Palestine, or the rights of political status enjoyed by Jews in any other country.

I should be grateful if you would bring this declaration to the knowledge of the Zionist Federation.

The letter, duly signed by the Foreign Secretary, became known as the Balfour Declaration. It was hailed by Jews all over the world as an act of national liberation comparable to the decree of Cyrus when that king permitted the captives in Persia to return to their homeland and rebuild their city and their temple. Significantly, when a Jewish state was proclaimed on May 14, 1948, Dr. Chaim Weizmann became its first President. World War I had prepared Palestine for the Jew.

Palestine and World War II

Under the dictatorial rulership of Germany by Adolph Hitler, 6,000,000 Jews died under an extermination program that was meant to be "the final solution" of the Jewish problem. Perhaps it was more than coincidence that most of the major military drives of World War II in Europe began on Saturday, the Jewish Sabbath. As an example, the panzer divisions of the Nazi army went into Vienna, Austria, on a Saturday. Jewish people by the thousand could have fled to a neighboring border for safety; but they still adhered to the old custom of limiting their travel on the Sabbath to "a Sabbath Day's journey" or about two-thirds of a mile, and would not carry a bag or umbrella on the Sabbath. Consequently they stayed in the streets of Vienna and were mowed down by the machine guns and run down by the tanks of the brutal invading army.

Such incidents were common over Europe in the wave of anti-Semitism that possessed the German government, and it caused the Jewish people once again to cry out for a homeland of their own. One said, "No matter how well we have at first been received, in the nations where we have gone, we have sooner or later become the victims of persecution and if we are going to die anyway, we will die in our own land." It appeared that whereas World War I prepared Palestine for the Jew, World War II prepared the Jew for Palestine.

In 1920 there were 58,000 Jews in Palestine. By 1967 their numbers had grown to 1,635,000 by the influx of immigrants from 107 countries.

The British mandate over the Holy Land was terminated on May 14, 1948, and on that same day the new State of Israel was proclaimed. As soon as the United Nations recognized Israel, war started between Arabs and Jews. It soon became clear that Israel could not be crushed, and an armistice was signed. But wars and rumors of wars have been the common lot of Israel since that time. Sensing an impending Egyptian attack, Israel invaded the Sinai in 1956. This quieted down when a cease-fire was arranged, with the United Nations forces patroling the area. However, when they were withdrawn war again broke out.

Once again, sensing an impending attack of great magnitude, Israel put her planes in the air on June 5, 1967, and wrecked 400 planes of the surrounding Arab armies in the first few hours of fighting. Two days later Israel's soldiers broke through the gates of the old city of Jerusalem and ran through Arab sniper fire to the Western Wall, the last remaining remnant of their temple, and hurled themselves weeping against those timeworn stones. General Moshe Dyan said, "We have returned to the holiest of our holy places. I give you my word we shall never be parted from it again." For 19 years the city had been divided, but now it was all in the possession of the Israelis for the first time in over 1,900 years.

The Jerusalem newspaper in one of its editorials carried the statement, "Jerusalem, Israel's eternal city and Capital, is not divided anymore. The Lord has brought about this day." With the taking of the entire city, hope began to rise that the Messiah would soon appear.

Plans for Temple Building

It seems apparent from the Scriptures that two temples are in Israel's future. One will be that in which Antichrist places his image and requires the worship of Israel to be directed to himself. The second is the millennial temple of which the prophet Ezekiel speaks in the last nine chapters of his Book. The immediate building of a temple is delayed chiefly because the original site is now occupied by a Moslem Mosque, commonly known as the Dome of the Rock. It stands squarely on the site of Solomon's Temple, and is second only to Mecca as the holiest place of the Muslim faith.

The Israeli historian, Dr. Israel Eldad, said, "We are at the stage where David was when he liberated Jerusalem. From that time until the construction of the Temple by Solomon, only one generation passed. So it will be with us."

When asked what would become of the Dome of the Rock, Dr. Eldad replied, "Who knows? Perhaps there will be an earthquake."

Reports of plans to build a temple in Israel have been increasing. In the halls of Jewish learning, temple knowledge is being emphasized to educate the people in proper temple worship.

According to an Associated Press story by George W. Cornell (*Pentecostal Evangel,* August 18, 1974), construction is due to begin soon on the first large central Jewish house of worship in Jerusalem since the destruction of the temple 1,904 years ago.

"No one is suggesting that this means the restoration of the temple," says Rabbi Maurie A. Jaffee, president of the Union of Israel Synagogues which is sponsoring the project. "But there are parallels."

Jewish pilgrims from all over the world may travel to Jerusalem to pray—just as they came to the temple centuries ago—in the new "Jerusalem Great Synagogue."

The new $10 million structure will be situated next to the Hechal Shlomo, Israel's chief rabbinical offices, just as the old temple adjoined the quarters of the religious council.

Other more ambitious Jews want to rebuild the temple on the original site. There are many obstacles to such a project at the present time, however. The Arabs will not stand idly by while their Dome of the Rock is removed, and the Jews will not disturb the shrine because it is unlawful in Israel to disturb any site sacred to any religion. They know from past history how tragic it is to have the symbols of faith desecrated.

Another obstacle comes from Christian sources. Knowing that the death of Christ was sufficient atonement, Christians see no reason to have a temple on earth where sacrifices are offered, although Ezekiel indicates that sacrifices will be reinstituted for memorial purposes.

Further objections have been raised by Jewish

theologians, who insist that Messiah must come first and regather the Jews, before they can go ahead with rebuilding the temple. Official rabbinical law at present forbids the Jews to touch the temple site. When they took the Wailing Wall in the Six-day War, they were told not to go farther into the area of the temple proper.

Still further objections are raised in that Israel lacks a proper priesthood to staff a temple. The Old Testament priesthood is extinct, or at least dormant. Furthermore, many of the reform Jews oppose animal sacrifices.

So we see there are Muslim, Christian, and Jewish objections standing in the way of temple construction at this time. However, the temple will be built, for prophecy must be fulfilled.

Because the Jewish nation is reborn in Palestine, and because ancient Jerusalem is once again under total Jewish control after 2,600 years, and because of the talk concerning a new temple, the most important sign of Jesus Christ's soon coming is before us.

The eyes of the world are upon Israel. Every day the news of that land is awaited by the nations of the world. Jesus said, "Jerusalem shall be trodden down of the Gentiles, until the times of the Gentiles be fulfilled" (Luke 21:24). Now Jerusalem is again a Jewish city and the Jews have vowed never to let it go. The Lord continued, "And when these things *begin to come to pass,* then look up, and lift up your heads; for your redemption draweth nigh" (v. 28).

A land is reborn, and a spiritual revival is on the way. The Conference on the Holy Spirit held in Jerusalem early in the spring of 1974 was attended by thousands of delegates from all over the world, including hundreds of Jewish people. When asked if the conference was making any impact upon the city or upon the governing heads of Israel, an eminent theologian replied, "I am certain that the heads of Israel know what is going on in the city, and are watching everything carefully. Furthermore, I have looked into the eyes of Jewish youth who have attended the conference and listened to the prophecies of the Old Testament being expounded and made relevant to contemporary events, and their eyes have shone with a new light and a new hope."

Yes, the stage is set. The key actors who will play out the drama of the last days are standing in the shadows waiting for their part in the play. But the Church of believing Christians will be taken up before the last act begins. Until that happens, God's plans for Israel are held in check. However, all indications point to imminent prophetic fulfillments such as the world has never seen. They cannot be postponed indefinitely.

10 The Eternal King

The long-range plan of God in which He is bringing many sons unto glory has for its grand culmination a world wherein dwelleth righteousness, with Jesus Christ as its chief object of worship and adoration. The Bible we now possess does not exhaust the wisdom and knowledge of our God. It is complete and sufficient in every way for the purpose of making the program of redemption known to humanity; but God, whose activities span the eternities past and future, has further plans to unfold when the present plan has run its course.

Paul's deepest writings are no doubt found in Ephesians, where he attempts to stretch the human imagination to plumb the wonders of God's program; and he states that God "hath raised us up together, and made us sit together in heavenly places in Christ Jesus: *that in the ages to come* he might show the exceeding riches of his grace, in his kindness toward us, through Christ Jesus" (Ephesians 2:6, 7).

"Ages to come." Think of it—one age after another

unfolding from the infinite riches of the knowledge and wisdom and love of God, wherein those who have been redeemed by the blood of Christ shall forever be learning about the wonders of God, and enjoying ever-deepening fellowship with the Creator and with one another.

It would appear from the Scriptures we now have that the present program of God from creation down to the close of the millennial reign of Jesus is confined to this planet Earth. Many countries are named in the Bible, others are referred to, and many are simply called "the heathen" or "the Gentiles"; but all is limited to activities and fulfillments in this small part of God's universe.

However, it is intimated that the plans of God beyond the Millennium include activities for the Church (the redeemed) in other parts of God's creation. While it is not good to endeavor to be wise beyond what is written and revealed, yet the inquisitive mind of man seeks to reason from a premise to a conclusion, for "God hath set eternity in his heart." With this in mind, we should note carefully the apostle's statement in Ephesians 3:9, 10 that God wishes "to make all men see what is the fellowship of the mystery, which from the beginning of the world hath been hid in God, who created all things by Jesus Christ: to the intent that now unto the principalities and powers in heavenly places might be known by the church the manifold wisdom of God," and Paul calls this "the eternal purpose which He purposed in Christ Jesus our Lord" (v.11).

Let us ask some questions of a philosophical nature. Is this earth, which is but a speck in the vast creation, to be the only place where Christ will rule over intelligent beings? Are there other world systems similar to ours where God is known and loved? Do the myriads of stars and galaxies that shine down upon us travel their courses devoid of the presence of intelligent creatures? Will they continue so until they burn themselves out, or does the Creator have a plan for them in ages to come? When the career of sin is forever settled and past, and when eternal righteousness is brought in, will the human race then be permitted to populate other worlds as it has populated this one? If the Church is the bride of Christ, and if Christ is the One by whom all worlds were made, is the Church to be forever limited to this present part of the creation?

The answer to such questions seems to be that the Church is destined for rulership with Christ over all worlds and dominions. Of course, there is room for much speculation when one contemplates the distant future, but the prophet Isaiah said, "Of the increase of his government and peace there shall be no end" (Isaiah 9:7), and this can be true only if the rulership of Christ leaps the bounds of this small planet Earth and continues to grow through ceaseless ages as myriads of other intelligences learn about God and bring glory and honor unto Him. However, this may be speculative, so we will not dwell on it. There are other certainties already revealed to us that are thrilling to contemplate.

The Bride's Future Home

The last two chapters of the Bible speak of future ages upon this earth. It is here that sin began among mankind. It is here that the plan of redemption was unfolded. It is here that the Saviour, God's Son, died for the sins of the whole world, and made a way back to fellowship with a holy God. Therefore God has chosen this part of His universe as the "home base" for any dealings He may have in the future with other galaxies.

We are taught that the whole creation as we know it, which has been marred by sin, will be remade. The Lord said, "Behold, I make all things new." Just as the world of Noah's day underwent a complete renovation and purging by water, so the world that now exists is reserved for a fiery bath, a renovation. It will not be annihilated, but will be given a changed form. All the works of man that have accumulated on this earth through the centuries will be burned up. All disease germs, all pollution, many seas of the world will disappear, and it shall be remade into a place fit not only for natural generations of men, but also for redeemed and glorified people.

Following such a renovation a most glorious event will take place. John describes it thus:

> I John saw the holy city, new Jerusalem, coming down from God out of heaven, prepared as a bride adorned for her husband (Revelation 21:2).

It is not the purpose of this book to describe the city of God, but some description of it must be given, for Jesus is its King, and the redeemed are the inhabitants.

The city itself is not heaven, but comes down from God out of heaven. Some commentators believe the city is already complete, having been built in ages past as God's capital city for the entire universe, while others believe it is in the process of construction. They infer this from Jesus' words, "I go to prepare a place for you." Some also believe that the completion of the city will be synchronized with the completion of the work of taking out from among the Gentiles a people for His name. What we really do know about it is that when it makes its appearance from heaven and comes down to earth, it will be "prepared as a bride adorned for her husband."

It will be a literal city and will literally descend to earth. It will radiate light like a precious stone. Everything in that city will speak to the inhabitants of the goodness, the protection, and the eternal salvation God has provided. The wall of the city is very significant. Walls were built around cities in ancient times for their protection. This "wall great and high" is significant of the fact that the Bride will be adequately protected throughout eternity. Into the garden of Eden came the serpent to deceive Eve, and to bring about the fall of the race, and the introduction of sin with all its attendant evils; but the wall of the city speaks of the fact that no serpent of evil will ever be permitted to enter the new Jerusalem. This wall will have 12 foundations and in them the names of the 12 apostles of the Lamb. How significant! For the Church is built upon the foundation of the apostles and prophets (Ephesians 2:20).

We are first made aware of such a city in the writings of the Old Testament. David had some faint knowledge of it when he wrote, "Beautiful for situation, the joy of the whole earth, is mount Zion, on the sides of the north, the city of the great King. God is known in her palaces for a refuge" (Psalm 48:2, 3).

Jesus spoke of the city by referring to the many manisions in the Father's house, and John's description of the city in the last of the Revelation is the most descriptive in any literature.

The idea of a City of God, radiant with His presence, goes back to patriarchal times. When God first began to form a people for himself, and called Abraham out of Ur of the Chaldees, it is said that Abraham "looked for a city which hath foundations, whose builder and maker is God" (Hebrews 11:10). The life of that ancient patriarch was often made tedious by days of moving. The tent had to be taken down, the possessions placed on the backs of beasts of burden, a new place of pasture found, and then there was the task of pitching the tents again and getting the possessions scattered about for proper use. Often he wished for permanence, some place to really settle down for a long period of time. He dreamed of a dwelling place that need never be taken down—one that had foundations to it; one from which he need never move. So the writer of Hebrews tells us that God is very mindful of the longings in the hearts of all Christian pilgrims. He "is not ashamed to be called their God: for he hath prepared for them a city" (Hebrews 11:16). The writer also refers to all believers as having come to Mt. Zion, and unto the city of the living God, the heavenly Jerusalem, and to innumerable hosts of angels. In the midst of toil and earthly pilgrimage the saints are ever encouraged to look forward to that which is permanent, restful, and without the tensions of earth.

The idea of a Holy City in the literature of Israel is closely connected with the choosing of Jerusalem as the dwelling place of God and the prophecies that relate to the ultimate glory of this city. Ezekiel's last nine chapters speak about the future glory of earthly Jerusalem, but he gives it geographic boundaries, and speaks of its altar, its priests, and its temple. The earthly Jerusalem, though leveled 22 times in historic battles and captivities, still exists because God has chosen to put His name there as the future capital for millennial times. But the Holy City that comes down from God out of heaven will be the future capital for the eternal ages.

Cities have been the despair of mankind and have become concentrated centers of evil. As cities get old, slum areas appear. Buildings decay, and in the hands of wicked men the city becomes a monster that levels all unique characteristics into a common mass. Yet the city remains the ideal of God, for the life of heaven is centered around a city with gates and walls, and boys and girls playing in the streets. However, God's ideal is a city without a police force, without a hospital, or a graveyard, where there is freedom from pain, and from worry, and from tears and death. That is why His city is called the Holy City. His own holy presence is especially there, and the people He allows into that eternal home "have washed their robes, and made them white in the blood of the Lamb" (Revelation 7:14).

John measured the Holy City in his vision, and at eight furlongs to the mile, found the city to measure 1,500 miles in each direction. The Holy of Holies of Solomon's Temple was a perfect cube of 20 cubits in each direction, and the Holy City is the perfect antitype of that room in the temple. It will be the Holy of Holies of the eternal future.

F. W. Boreham, the famous pastor and author of Australia, had an engineer in his parish named Tammas who did some calculating, using as a premise the dimensions and information given in the Scriptures. A city of 12,000 furlongs in each direction would have 2,250,000 square miles. Adelaide, Australia, is exactly one square mile, so the Holy City would be 2,250,000 times as large as Adelaide. London, England, covers 140 square miles, so the Holy City would be about 16,000 times as large as London. It would be

20 times as large as all New Zealand, 10 times as big as Germany, 10 times as large as all of France, 40 times larger than England, larger than all of India. Using the number of people per square mile in London as a guide, the Holy City could take care of over 100 billion people, or about 30 times the present population of the globe.

When speaking of the Holy City, Horatius Bonar had this to say:

> Fit metropolis of the new earth, wherein dwelleth righteousness . . . how eagerly should we look for it! The right of citizenship is to be had now, and they who are to dwell in it are not angels, but men; not the unfallen, but the fallen. It is as such that we apply for the freedom of the city. He who is its Builder and Maker gives it freely. He who is its Prince, whose blood has bought and opened it, gives it freely. He waits to receive applications. He entreats men to apply. He announces that whosoever will only take Him at His word, and trust Him for entrance into it, shall have it. He specially proclaims to us His own sacrifice, His infinite propitiation, His divine bloodshedding on the Cross, and gives us to know that whosoever will receive the testimony to this great work of atonement shall enter in through the gates into the city. It is the Blood that brings us to the mercy seat; it is the Blood that brings us into the city. It will be a joy to enter that joyous city . . . and we beseech you now to make sure of your citizenship, by making sure of your connection with the King . . . for he who has the King has the city. (Quoted in *Prophecy Made Plain* by Carl Johnson. Moody Press.)

The unveiling of this city does not belong to this world now, nor to millennial days, but to the new heavens and new earth. It will be the final consummation of all prophetic utterance, and the climax to all the revelations we now have from God. Whatever may have been the vague dreams of the classical writers of Greece or of non-Christian mystics regarding a paradise of the future, this is the one account that is more beautiful than anything ever penned by writers without divine inspiration, but it is made sure to us because it all relates to and derives from the purposes of God accomplished in Jesus Christ our eternal Redeemer.

The late Dr. Donald Grey Barnhouse declared, "Christ is so wonderful that God determined that He was going to people the universe with an incredibly vast number of replicas of Christ, and we are the raw material of that plan."

What wonders await the child of God! His servants shall see His face. He will no longer be withdrawn from us so that we must live by faith alone, but as the tangible and personal contacts of this world are real, so will be our experiences with a personal Christ in our eternal home. And because of the marvels of the living Word, and the power of the Blood, and the ministry of the Holy Spirit, multiplied millions will be there as winsome as He is, for "we shall be like him, for we shall see him as he is."

The city has 12 gates, and at the gates are 12 angels, and the names of the 12 tribes of Israel are written upon the gates. Being built in heaven, it is no doubt built for conditions that exist there, and so it may prove to be quite different from what, with our present knowledge and understanding, we might expect. But some of the things now taking place every day upon this planet were supposed a few years ago to be so contrary to good reason and common sense that the possibility of their existence was not even suggested, such as radio, television, jet travel, computers, and myriads of appliances. Yet God is building a city that will be the home of the redeemed, and it will contain things that are beyond our conception today. Someone has said that the city will contain nothing that should not be there, and will include every possible item that will make for the eternal happiness of God's people.

The city is described as being of pure gold, like unto clear glass, a symbol of the divine righteousness. All Christians are "partakers of the divine nature," and John said, "It doth not yet appear what we shall be: but we know that, when he shall appear, we shall be like him; for we shall see him as he is" (1 John 3:2). No such gold as the gold out of which the home of the Bride is made has ever been known on earth; but God did not exhaust His resources when He made the gold of earth. This gold is gold of heaven, superior to anything we now know.

There are brief passages in the Scriptures that indicate that this earth, after its renovation by fire, shall be repopulated with people who live in their natural generations, in a pure state, apart from sin, and shall be able to enter and have access to the Holy City, "and shall bring the glory and honor of the nations into it."

Yes, the future home of the Christians will be, without doubt, the most beautiful home in the entire universe.

Future Travel

Though the Holy City will be home for the redeemed, it does not follow that we shall be confined to the city. There can be no doubt that the redeemed will enjoy all of God's wondrous works. Where David said, "The heavens declare the glory of God; and the firmament showeth his handiwork" (Psalm 19:1), the word *handiwork* comes from a root word meaning handmade, such as that produced by a woman knitting, or tatting, or crocheting. The heavens are the work of God's fingers, and they shall be seen in their beauty by the redeemed in future ages.

We have already sent men into space with the

sophisticated hardware of modern technology, with boom and blast and fire. God has an easier way. The glorified bodies of the redeemed will not be subject to heat or cold or to the power of gravity. As Enoch went up, and as Elijah was caught up by a whirlwind, and as Jesus ascended quietly and calmly into the heavenly world, a similar privilege will be enjoyed by the saints with their glorified bodies. This is the import of the verse, "We shall change our vile body, that it may be fashioned like unto his glorious body" (Philippians 3:21). Whether true or not, it has been suggested that travel will be "with the speed of thought"—faster than the speed of light—speeds unapproachable by present human ability. And perhaps this may be true in order that the redeemed may enjoy and visit the unlimited creation of our God.

Future Pleasure

From the very fact of our mortality, the fondest dreams and hopes of mankind are too often cut short without being realized. There are lofty ambitions in every heart that could take unnumbered years to explore, but the Grim Reaper cuts a man down in his prime and his ambition is never accomplished. Think of the astronomer who would like to pursue a study of the heavens, but whose ambition is cut short by death. Consider the geologist, or the botanist, who delights in the pursuit of his field of knowledge, but who is forced to give it up while still in his prime. Is this to be the condititon of the human spirit forever? No, for the God who put these urges within us will no doubt allow us to enjoy the pursuit of knowledge in these chosen fields as long as our hearts desire.

At a fellowship meeting an elderly man rose to testify. He had lived for God many years and was a man of much prayer. He related that one evening after he had retired an angel of God took him by the hand, led him down the stairs of his home, and into the gardens of God. Perhaps it was a vision or dream. He said he was amazed at the greenery, the foliage, the beauty of the landscape, in that heavenly land to which the angel took him; and in his testimony he continued to repeat in an amazed manner, "There was not a faded leaf . . . there was not a faded leaf."

Another child of God related how she loved music, especially choirs and group singing where there is three- and four-part harmony. In a dream one night she heard a heavenly choir sing, and stated "there were 30 to 40 parts intermingling in a symphony of melody and harmony such as earth has never heard."

Still another child of God related how he had a vision of the Marriage Supper of the Lamb, and saw the tables spread with all manner of delectable foods. Angels served, and saints of the centuries enjoyed one another's fellowship at the tables. The Lord was present, enjoying the supper with His people. He related how the tablecloth seemed to have an inherent light of its own, and the tableware was finer than that used by kings of earth.

It is easy to make more of the details of a vision than is warranted at times, but these testimonies, and many others similar to them, indicate God has provided a marvelous degree of pleasure for His people.

The beauty of the eternal age staggers the imagination. It is not wise to speculate wildly about its details, but it is wise to so live that when that time comes, we may enjoy it to the full. In this life we live by faith. We understand spiritual things with our heart, and enjoy them according to our measure of faith and according to the way we follow on to know the Lord.

Here in this life our ears hear profanity, worldly

music, evil speaking. Our bodies are subject to aches, pains, sicknesses, diseases. In the midst of all this we are asked "to walk in the light as he is in the light." How immense our joy will be when our eyes behold Him and all He has. Our ears will hear His voice . . . our bodies shall be fashioned like His own . . . and we shall learn of the riches of His grace forever.

Future Fellowship

A friend of Fanny Crosby was once sitting with her on the porch describing a beautiful sunset. He mentioned how large the sun looked, its brilliant color, its spreading rays of light, the formation of the clouds at the moment. Mrs. Crosby said, "I cannot see the sunset you are describing for I am blind; but when my eyes are opened, the first face I shall ever see is the face of Jesus."

Such has been the yearning and longing of the believers of all time. Fellowship with Jesus Christ, the Son of God, will be our chief delight in the heavenly world.

We should also remember that we shall have the privilege of knowing in a very personal manner others whom we have read about in the Word of God. The patriarchs, the prophets, the myriads of godly people whose words and deeds are recorded in both the Old and New Testaments, the converts of unnumbered evangelistic crusades, the fruit gleaned unto God by pastoral efforts. The presence of these in the eternal ages shall make the years most blessed as we have fellowship together without any time limit to worry us. Sickness and tragedy shall never cut that fellowship short.

Every family has had the sore trial of bereavement, the breaking of earthly ties with loved ones. We have established ceremonies and composed special hymns for such occasions, but they are always difficult times, for death is an enemy, and in death there is no respect of persons. However, the Christian is told not to sorrow as those who have no hope. Here we have the glorious implication that the Christian has everything to hope for, since the resurrection of Jesus Christ from the dead is the harbinger of a glorious resurrection for all who sleep in Jesus. We shall see our Christian loved ones again. This was the faith of the early saints, and over the tombs of many was written, "A temporary rest is granted you." And when we see them again in the resurrection, it will be with the knowledge that partings are forever over.

Jesus is coming again. Events in our world at the present time indicate that the Daystar is rising, for the Lord himself has born testimony to these things, and He it is who says, "Surely I come quickly."

The coming of the Lord will be the solution to the world's problems. These problems will never be solved until He shall come. Until then there will be wars, rumors of wars, confusion, chaos, perils, and perplexities. There will be atheism and apostasy, trouble and tribulation. But when Christ comes, peace will prevail. Swords will be beaten into ploughshares, and spears into pruning hooks, and the nations will learn war no more. Righteousness will be dominant in the earth. Poverty will disappear. The golden age to which humanity has been looking forward will then dawn. Men will wonder as they look back to the days in which we live how men and women could ever have been so foolish and so wicked as to spend their time and devote their energies to the gruesome task of spreading death and destruction and desolation in the earth. Forever and ever men will be able to look back upon the darkness of this world as an object lesson that it never pays to live without God. The centuries of godlessness on this earth have no doubt been a picture to wondering angels of the high cost of rebellion.

The cry of the Church and of the whole creation is for Christ to come. Come, Lord Jesus! Come quickly!

> Come, then, and added to Thy many crowns
> Receive yet one, the crown of all the earth,
> Thou who alone art worthy! It was Thine
> By ancient covenant, ere nature's birth;
> And Thou hast made it Thine by purchase since,
> And overpaid its value with Thy blood.
> Thy saints proclaim Thee King, and in their hearts
> Thy title is engraven with a pen
> Dipped in the fountain of eternal love.
>
> —William Cowper, in "The Task"